T.D. JAKES

SIX PILLARS FROM EPHESIANS

Loved By God

THE SPIRITUAL WEALTH OF THE BELIEVER

ALBURY PUBLISHING
Tulsa, Oklahoma

Unless otherwise indicated, all Scripture quotations are taken from the *King James Version* of the Holy Bible.

The Scripture quotation marked NKJV is taken from the *New King James Version* of the Bible. Copyright © 1979, 1980, 1982, Thomas Nelson, Inc., Publishers.

2nd Printing

Six Pillars From Ephesians: Loved by God
The Spiritual Wealth of the Believer
ISBN 1-57778-107-4
Copyright © 2000 by T. D. Jakes
T. D. Jakes Ministries
International Communications Center
P. O. Box 75211
Dallas, Texas 75211

Published by ALBURY PUBLISHING
P. O. Box 470406
Tulsa, Oklahoma 74147-0406

CONTENTS

℧

LOVED BY GOD
THE SPIRITUAL WEALTH OF THE BELIEVER

℧

INTRODUCTION

The Ephesians understood wealth — great wealth.

Ephesus was a city with marble streets, mosaic sidewalks, a massive temple that was considered one of the wonders of the Greek world, a busy port, a popular athletic arena, one of the finest libraries in the first century, and villas that were filled with artwork, tapestries, silks, and exotic birds and animals. Even today, the coliseum at Ephesus is considered one of the finest performing centers in the world.

Caravans from the east routinely ended their journeys at Ephesus, and ships from ports throughout the Mediterranean brought the riches of Egypt, Rome, Greece, Spain, and northern Africa. Anything of natural wealth that a person might desire could be purchased or enjoyed to excess in Ephesus.

Yes, the Ephesians understood wealth, but the apostle Paul came to town and blew their minds by presenting a type of wealth they had never encountered before. Paul brought the riches of heaven. He presented to them the God of all riches, the God who gave His only begotten Son, His most precious possession.

We can discover just how precious Jesus was to God when we examine the Greek word translated "only begotten," which is *monogenes*, a compound word. *Mono* means "only," and *ginomai* means "to be." Jesus was "the only one to be" — the only one of a kind who ever existed. He was highly precious and of exceeding value to God because He was extremely rare. There was no one like Him and no one else in His category. God's willingness to share and sacrifice for us this wholly unique treasure, His only begotten Son, was the supreme expression of His love for us.

The wealth the apostle Paul brought to Ephesus is the same wealth the book of Ephesians presents to all people: Jesus Christ. In Him is everything a human being could ever dream of, hope for, or desire — and more.

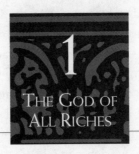

1

THE GOD OF ALL RICHES

There has never been a time in history where most people did not believe that possessing great wealth was the key to happiness. Yet time and time again we have seen millionaires and billionaires live miserable lives and even kill themselves. We have watched their children wander through life aimlessly, self-destruct, and even use their wealth to destroy others. Why? Because their wealth was in temporal things and not in eternal blessings.

Material wealth is not an evil in and of itself. Ten dollars in the hands of a criminal or a pastor is still ten dollars, and ten dollars in the hands of that pastor can do great good! The Bible says it is the *love* of money that is the root of all evil. (See 1 Timothy 6:10.) When we love money, we are consumed with making it, multiplying it, and keeping it. But the truth is, it has us by the throat and our lives are meaningless.

Mankind must connect to the God of all riches to truly enjoy — and to avoid being controlled and owned by — material wealth. Thank God, through Jesus Christ, we can connect! And when that divine connection takes place and we are gloriously born again, the Holy Spirit comes to dwell in our hearts and we begin the adventure of the truly privileged: discovering our riches in Christ.

KNOWING OUR SOURCE

To be convinced that we are about to receive great riches, we must be convinced that the person *giving* the riches to us is capable of doing so. We certainly know that any time a person writes a check and hands it to us, the check is only as good as the check-writer's ability to pay. We must know that they possess the amount in the bank that is written on the slip of paper handed to us.

As children of God, we must know that our heavenly Father possesses everything we need in life, a promise He makes to us from cover to cover, throughout the Bible. Therefore, Paul opens his letter to the Ephesians by declaring the grace, resources, and power of God, the author of all wealth. It is vitally important for us to know that the verses at the beginning of chapter 1 are speaking distinctly and primarily of God the Father and

His redemptive plan and work. From "Blessed be the God and Father" in verse 3 through verse 14, "unto the praise of his glory," the Holy Spirit is revealing to us the majesty, riches, and power of Almighty God, the Father of our Lord Jesus Christ. Although the revelation of the Father God impacts our lives significantly and dynamically for all time, this particular passage is not about us. This passage is about *Him* — His glory and His grace.

> *Paul, an apostle of Jesus Christ by the will of God, to the saints which are at Ephesus, and to the faithful in Christ Jesus:*
> *Grace be to you, and peace, from God our Father, and from the Lord Jesus Christ.*
> *Blessed be the God and Father of our Lord Jesus Christ, who hath blessed us with all spiritual blessings in heavenly places in Christ.*
>
> EPHESIANS 1:1-3

"Blessed be the God and Father of our Lord Jesus Christ." Paul considers the foundation for all of our blessings in Christ to be this fact: *God* is blessed. He is not frail, impoverished, or impotent. He has every resource at His disposal, both things seen and unseen. Nothing lies beyond His ownership. A person or a group of people may think they own or control certain resources, but ultimately, it is God who owns those resources and who has temporarily allowed man to use them.

God is all-powerful. He is fully capable and able in all situations, at all times, and regardless of circumstance to exert control over His resources. God has authority over all things. He can and will do what He *says* He can and will do when it comes to blessings and the transfer of wealth.

Mining companies don't truly *own* the gold and silver and other precious stones and metals of this earth.

Oil companies don't truly *own* the oil and gas resources of the earth.

Man can never *own* any of the earth's resources because all resources are *created* by God.

The One who creates is the one who owns!

Who owns ideas?

Who owns creativity?

Who owns motivation or enthusiasm?

Who owns ability?

Who owns talents?

Who created these capacities in man?

God did! What God creates, God owns. He imparts these resources to people and allows them to use His resources, but He never relinquishes ownership over His resources. Behind every transaction and every transfer of wealth on this earth are ability, ideas, invention, innovation, and energy. All are owned by God, because all are created by God and imparted by God.

The devil doesn't own anything he thinks he owns.

The gang doesn't own your neighborhood.

The criminal doesn't own what he steals.

God may have allowed a transfer of authority over certain resources temporarily, but it is always *God* who allows that transfer. Nothing and nobody can force the hand of God or lay rightful claim to the things He has created. However, we are God's children, and He delights in blessing His own. It is His desire to show us all His kingdom has to offer us.

When we are born again, we become God's children; we are His family. And in any family, there is a difference between what outsiders know about the family versus what family members know. My sons and daughters know things about me — what I have, what I want, and what I do — that the outside world never sees and can never know. In the same way, being a part of the family of God automatically brings with it the privilege of knowing God in an intimate, family way.

The point I'm making is that when you are a child of God, you have the awesome honor of gazing upon the riches of your Father's wealth. And, because you know what He has, your expectation from Him and your confidence in Him are enhanced. My children fully expect that when they come to me and ask for money, I will give it to them. They never question if I have it, how I'm going to get it, or where it comes from — they just know I'll give it to them. However, being a good father, I will exercise restraint at times. Thus, I am not only good *to* them, but I am good *for* them. And that is how God is to us.

God often withholds blessing and prosperity from us for a season in order to temper our character or to correct flawed behavior. Then, when the blessing comes, we will be mature enough to handle it. If He gave it to us prematurely, it could destroy us. This is such an important concept for believers to understand. Without that understanding, it is easy to become discouraged and even turn from God in anger if, when we exercise our faith with all expectancy and confidence in God to give us what we have requested, it does not come to us when we think we should have it. However, if our faith in God's wisdom to direct our lives is greater than our personal agenda, we will hold on tenaciously to our faith in His promise, grow up, and wait patiently for the blessing to come.

Once we know that God is the benevolent and wise owner of everything, then we ask the question, "Well, just *what* does He own?" As family, we want to know just how far our inheritance extends! The truth that must sink into our spirits is: *Blessed be God!* God is blessed. Anything that we perceive to be a blessing in heaven or on this earth, God *is* that, *has* that, or *does* that to the infinite degree! Any resource that is related to value or wealth belongs to, comes from, and is controlled by God, our Father, who desires to bless *us*.

The perception we have about the grandeur and blessedness of God becomes the reservoir from which we draw the refreshing waters of God's blessings for our lives. And knowing the blessings of God provokes us to worship. Paul is not only telling us that God is blessed, *he is blessing God.* Blessed be God!

Let me interject here that this is the reason why thanksgiving, praise, and worship are so important to us. The more we worship God, the more He is *magnified* in our hearts, where we know Him as the Father who loves us, and our minds, where we know Him as the Supplier of our needs. And when He appears great and awesome to us, our problems will wither and become microscopic before Him. It is much easier for us to believe God can and will meet our needs and resolve our problems when He towers over our difficulties and overwhelms us with His compassion.

FAITH IS THE RECEIVER OF WEALTH

Our faith grows stronger as we perceive God's greatness as both sovereign and loving heavenly

Father. Then we become more receptive to His blessings because God always responds to *faith*. Time and again we read in the Scriptures that Jesus said to those who came to Him for miracles of healing and deliverance, "As you have believed, it will be done to you" and "Your faith has made you whole."

> **T**hen touched he their eyes, saying, According to your faith be it unto you.
>
> MATTHEW 9:29

> **A**nd Jesus said unto the centurion, Go thy way; and as thou hast believed, so be it done unto thee. And his servant was healed in the selfsame hour.
>
> MATTHEW 8:13

Faith is the catalyst that accelerates the divine transfer of wealth to us as believers in Christ Jesus. Faith is what motivates God to release His resources on our behalf, and faith conditions us to receive His wealth and to record or mark on our assets page that the deposit has cleared and the funds are available for use.

Having faith to believe God *wants* to bless us is another great challenge we have in receiving His blessings. Although it is easier to receive all God desires to give us when we know and are assured of His vast and unending wealth, if we see God without the *desire* to transfer His resources to us, our faith to believe and receive is cut off. We are going to see

God as rich, but indifferent, aloof, and unconcerned. When this is our perception, our faith is diminished, our prayers are muttered halfheartedly, our tenacity weakens, and we have no ability to receive miracles from God.

We must build ourselves up on our most holy faith by praying in the Spirit (see Jude 20) and continually feeding our spirits and renewing our minds with the Word of God, because faith comes by hearing the Word and strengthens our inner man. (See Romans 10:17.) The Holy Spirit and the Word are the dynamic duo God has given us to become superheroes of faith, to become like Jesus. Jesus had no problem either receiving or utilizing all the riches His Father had already provided for Him during His time on earth. God had made all provision ready for Jesus even before He was conceived in Mary's womb, and Jesus was well aware of that fact.

A DONE DEAL

Blessed be the God and Father of our Lord Jesus Christ, who hath blessed us with all spiritual blessings in heavenly places in Christ.

EPHESIANS 1:3 (EMPHASIS MINE)

15

Paul said, "Blessed be the God and Father of our Lord Jesus Christ, who *hath* blessed us." "Hath" is not a word that relates to the "sweet by-and-by" or "somewhere on the other side." "Hath" is past tense. The blessings God has prepared for us have already been put into place. This is a finished work. It is complete, settled, over, and done with. The blessings of God are not rooted in our expectation or hope, but in a heaven reality. From God's viewpoint, we possess the land of blessing right now. All of the blessings we can ever receive from God have already been created, established, and are in a "holding pattern," just waiting for us to possess them. We tend to look at the blessings of the Lord as "potentially ours," but God sees them as "possessively ours."

We are like Joshua, when he stood on the banks of the Jordan looking over into the promised land. The Lord told him that every piece of land where he would put his foot had already been given to him. (See Joshua 1:3.) Joshua hadn't crossed the Jordan River yet. He wasn't living in the land. Enemies were still living there, and there were battles ahead. But the fact was, the land belonged to Joshua and the Israelites. God had given it to them — past tense, done deal, established work.

Let's suppose that I said to my son, "That car out in the driveway is yours, Son. Here are the keys. Go drive it away." Does that car belong to my son? Yes. Has he possessed it yet? No. Can he possess it if he goes out to it, gets in it, turns the key in the ignition, and drives away? Yes.

It sounds like a paradox to say, "It's yours" and then to say, "Go take it," but that's the position God puts us in. The problem many people have is that they don't *know* what is already theirs. Before my son would go out and get in that car and drive away, he would have to know the truth of what I said to him, "Son, that car is your car. I have given it to you." He would have to believe the car was owned by me in the first place, believe I had the power to give it to him, and then believe I wanted to give it to him.

Do you believe God owns what you need?

Do you believe God has the power to give you what you need?

Do you believe He wants to meet your needs?

The first step to possessing our inheritance is *knowing* and *believing* God has what we need. The second step is personally taking possession of what has been decreed, bequeathed, or given to us. Most believers seem to spend their entire lives reading the will and shouting over the contract, but never moving out and obtaining what God has given them. We sing about the promises, shout about them, talk about them, write music about them, teach about them, read about them — yet never *live* in them. Why? Because we aren't willing to cross over the river and fight the spiritual battles that must be fought in order for us to take possession of what is rightfully ours.

Everything you could possibly need is available to you and to the full measure you could ever desire it. Let me assure you today, you are rich beyond measure! But you still have to lay hold of what God has promised to you and what God has already given to you. God said to Joshua,

> **Be** *strong and of a good courage; be not afraid, neither be thou dismayed: for the Lord thy God is with thee whithersoever thou goest.*

JOSHUA 1:9

Joshua had work to do. It was going to take strength and courage to occupy a land infested with enemies. What gave Joshua the strength and courage? Knowing that the Lord was with him and that He had already assured his victory in taking possession of the land. It is knowing God that gives us the strength and courage we need to step out in faith and obtain the wealth He has for us. The degree of our faith is based upon our intimacy with our heavenly Father.

It is time for us to know with certainty that no matter what happens around us, the God of all riches has the blessings and desires with all His heart to give them to us. We must be completely assured and confident that He is going to make our efforts successful as we obey Him and fight the battles to obtain all that He has for us. Tremendous, life-changing, abundant blessings are waiting for us, if we will only pursue them and possess them in faith.

Blessed be the God and Father of our Lord Jesus Christ, who hath blessed us with all spiritual blessings in heavenly places in Christ.

EPHESIANS 1:3

We know that God's wealth includes everything in the universe that He created, but this verse in Ephesians means much more and goes far beyond anything we can perceive with our senses or imagine with our mind. This verse calls us to reach an understanding of our wealth that puts our entire life in proper perspective: The blessings God has provided for us in heavenly places in Christ are first and foremost *spiritual blessings.*

Paul is not talking about prosperity in terms of dollars and cents, the clothes we wear, the homes we live in, or the cars we drive. He is talking about spiritual blessings. Spiritual blessings, however, are *related* to material, physical, financial, emotional, and mental blessings. As believers, we are instructed to begin with and always focus on the spiritual bless-ings. Then, it is the outworking of those spiritual blessings that produces an abundant life in the practical and material realm in which we live.

What many believers in Christ Jesus haven't fully recognized is that all natural and material blessings are the fruit of spiritual blessings. The root of all blessing lies in the spirit realm. A fruit tree cannot bear fruit if it has no root. If the trunk of the tree is cut away from its roots, that chunk of wood has no potential for bearing fruit, nor do its leaves and branches. The life of a tree flows from the hidden, unseen root system that lies under the soil. Life flows up into the visible tree out of the invisible depths of the soil, and the branches produce fruit that is good, beneficial, and abundant.

In like manner, our spiritual life is invisible and hidden within. The life that Christ Jesus imparts to us in the invisible recesses of our heart flows up into the visible realm and produces fruit which can be seen. The fruit of the Spirit is love, joy, peace, patience, gentleness, goodness, faith, humility, and self-control. The person who is rich in spirit is the person who is able to produce the fruit that will result in all of the physical and natural blessings necessary for living like Jesus on this earth.

Understanding, moving into, and possessing spiritual blessings increase your capacity to receive all of the natural and physical blessings of this life. Spiritual blessings are the key to achieving fullness of life.

ETERNAL BLESSINGS

> **W**hile we look not at the things which are seen, but at the things which are not seen: for the things which are seen are temporal; but the things which are not seen are eternal.
>
> 2 CORINTHIANS 4:18

In the last chapter, we saw that God has already blessed us with all spiritual blessings. This concept is easy to understand once we see that spiritual blessings are *eternal*. They existed before we did, and when we became God's child, He deposited them into our new, recreated spirit in the form of the Holy Spirit.

Are you aware that all of the spiritual blessings you will ever need or desire are already resident inside you? They have already been imparted to you. You received them the moment you accepted Jesus Christ as your Savior. All spiritual blessings — the full-to-overflowing bounty of all that God is and has for you — is now resident in you because the Holy Spirit lives in you!

Spiritual blessings last forever, because they emanate from the Holy Spirit, who is eternal. But natural blessings are for a season and are temporary, no matter how great or wonderful they may seem to us at the time. Therefore, we must always guard our hearts and minds to maintain godly priorities. Our treasure should be found in God and not in things. The Bible is very clear on this point. Jesus said,

> *Lay not up for yourselves treasures upon earth, where moth and rust doth corrupt, and where thieves break through and steal:*
>
> *But lay up for yourselves treasures in heaven, where neither moth nor rust doth corrupt, and where thieves do not break through nor steal:*
>
> *For where your treasure is, there will your heart be also.*
>
> MATTHEW 6:19-21

No matter what form of physical or material treasure we may possess, a greater treasure is always going to be the spiritual treasures of God. Notice the balance in what Jesus teaches:

> *Therefore take no thought, saying, What shall we eat? or, What shall we drink? or, Where withal shall we be clothed?*
>
> *(For after all these things do the Gentiles seek:) for your heavenly Father knoweth that ye have need of all these things.*

But seek ye first the kingdom of God, and his right-
eousness; and all these things shall be added unto you.

MATTHEW 6:31-33

In the time in which we live, to be "anxious" means to be eager or excited about something. We say, for instance, "I am anxious for my guests to arrive." However, in the Greek text, the word "anxious" has another meaning. It comes from the Greek word *merimnao*, which means "to be unduly concerned, to have anxiety, or to worry about something."

Jesus emphatically tells us many times in the gospels that we are not to be anxious or to worry about anything in life. God knows what we need and it is His delight to supply what we need. If spiritual blessings are our top priority and the kingdom of God is our number-one pursuit, God will take care of all the material things that concern us without any anxiety or frustration on our part. The natural blessings flow from the spiritual blessings, and the spiritual blessings flow from the vast and infinite reservoir of God's blessedness.

Every good gift and every perfect gift is from above,
and cometh down from the Father of lights, with whom
is no variableness, neither shadow of turning.

JAMES 1:17

Every blessing begins with God, and for us to obtain His blessings, we must perceive, receive, and

25

possess them first in the spirit realm from Him. We must turn from our personal agendas, concerns, and selfish desires, and worship Him in spirit and in truth in everything we think, say, and do. By this, we are choosing to connect with the eternal God, not the temporal world. We are literally plugging ourselves into His eternal thoughts and ways, which causes us to act and behave according to His will. When we give Him ourselves completely and carry out His plan for our lives with everything in our being, He can easily pour His blessings upon our lives.

THREE SPIRITUAL BLESSINGS

Before we go any further, I want us to examine three spiritual blessings that are the foundation of all our wealth as believers: faith, grace, and strength. Just a simple, rudimentary understanding of these three powerful principles of the Christian life will allow any believer to walk in God's abundance and blessing.

Faith. All the faith we need has already been allocated to us and deposited in us. The Bible tells us that God has dealt to every man the measure of faith.

> **F**or I say, through the grace given unto me, to every man that is among you...God hath dealt to every man the measure of faith.
>
> ROMANS 12:3

We already have all the faith we need! Furthermore, we have the agent of faith working in us — the Holy Spirit of God. In Jude 20, we are instructed to pray in the Holy Ghost, because this strengthens and builds our faith. In Romans 10:17, we are told that faith rises up and expands in our hearts as we read, hear, and study God's Word. Faith is what moves God. Faith is our key to accessing the full power of God, like a key in the ignition of a vehicle that ignites the engine. Our faith ignites the heart of God and releases His love, wisdom, power, and presence into any situation or circumstance.

Grace. Grace is the attitude of God that causes His love to transcend our sin and deliver to us the full measure of His support and work. Grace means that we don't have to strive and struggle through this life to prove ourselves and to make it on our own. We no longer have to live in oppression or depression or any other kind of "press," because God has given us His favor. His grace is what enables us to move forward and run the race with confidence and without any sense of shame or condemnation, because we know His love for us is unconditional.

But where sin abounded, grace did much more abound.

ROMANS 5:20

Who hath saved us, and called us with an holy calling, not according to our works, but according to

27

his own purpose and grace, which was given us in
Christ Jesus before the world began.

2 TIMOTHY 1:9

By *whom also we have access by faith into this*
grace wherein we stand, and rejoice in hope of the
glory of God.

ROMANS 5:2

Throughout the epistles we find verse after verse reminding us that God's grace is what transforms us, renews us, and makes us strong in faith. Our part is not to struggle to make things happen. Our part is to acknowledge the grace of God and take joy as the Holy Spirit makes things happen in us and through us and in others. What a gift this is to us!

Make no mistake, however, we are not freed from work or effort! That is not what grace means. When we understand God's grace, we have the confidence and assurance to do the work of the kingdom, knowing that God's blessing is upon us.

Grace is also the power that enables us to endure and progress through insufferable challenges. Paul knew this and honestly testified of the empowering of grace in 2 Corinthians 12:8-10 concerning his "thorn in the flesh." Have you ever had a thorn in your flesh, such as a splinter in your finger or a cactus needle stuck in your leg? It is very painful and incredibly distressing! It won't kill you, but it will make your life miserable until it is removed. Paul's thorn was the same type of situation. This thorn would not kill him, but it was a constant source of vexation and frustration to his ministry. In the end, however, he found God's grace to be sufficient. The grace of God undergirded his faith and spurred him on to persevere through every battle and gain the victory.

In Acts 20:32, when Paul makes his tearful and emotional good-bye to the Ephesian leaders, he commends them to "the word of his grace, which is able to build you up." Why did he commend them to "the word of his grace, which is able to build you up"? Because in verses 28-31 he has warned them that after his departure, vicious wolves are going to try to infiltrate their flocks and steal and destroy their sheep. Only "the word of his grace" will keep the Ephesian church built up and strong enough in God to identify the wolves and dispel them from their midst.

The effect of Paul's words on the Ephesian leaders in Acts 20 proved potent and powerful. We know they took his commendation to heart and immediately acted upon it, and we see that the grace with which Paul greeted them in Ephesians 1:2 was the persevering strength that enabled them to receive Jesus' commendation in Revelation 2:2-3:

I know thy works, and thy labour, and thy patience, and how thou canst not bear them which are evil: and thou hast tried them which say they are apostles, and are not, and hast found them liars:

And hast borne, and hast patience, and for my name's sake hast laboured, and hast not fainted.

Grace kept the Ephesians free of wolves and empowered them to bear every burden patiently, and it will do the same for us today. Grace, knowing and experiencing the favor and work of God in our lives, enables us to persevere and overcome otherwise insurmountable harassments and obstacles.

Strength. Our strength comes from the omnipotent, all-powerful Holy Spirit who resides within us. His strength allows us to stand in times of difficulty, endure all heartache and sorrow, resist all temptation, and remain steadfast in faith. The Holy Spirit actually uses difficult times to strengthen us for future and greater blessings. Each of us is in the process of being fashioned into a mighty pillar in the temple of our Lord!

For our light affliction, which is but for a moment, worketh for us a far more exceeding and eternal weight of glory.

2 CORINTHIANS 4:17

We can never forget that what God has called us to do is beyond our abilities, talents, and strength. Consequently, God infuses in us divine enablement, the supernatural energy to do superhuman exploits for the kingdom. Paul got to the place where he actually looked forward to trials and testings which challenged his natural strength and ability. In one particular situation, he asked the Lord three times to remove what he called a "thorn in the flesh." Here is Jesus' reply and Paul's response to it:

> **A**nd he said unto me, My grace is sufficient for thee: for my strength is made perfect in weakness. Most gladly therefore will I rather glory in my infirmities, that the power of Christ may rest upon me.
>
> Therefore I take pleasure in infirmities, in reproaches, in necessities, in persecutions, in distresses for Christ's sake: for when I am weak, then am I strong.
>
> 2 CORINTHIANS 12:9-10

When terrible and difficult things happen to us, if we will turn to Jesus and trust in Him, He will fill us with His strength to carry on and go to the next level. And after a few experiences of being filled with the strength of God to persevere, the mere thought of doing anything in our own strength again becomes repugnant to us! God's strength is far superior.

Faith. Grace. Strength. These three blessings of God are an unbeatable combination: the ability to believe...the confidence to act...and the power to persevere. Everything becomes accessible and possible when these spiritual blessings are activated in us!

THE OUTWARD WORKING
OF INWARD WEALTH

When we face a problem, the Lord doesn't jump up from His throne in heaven and cry, "Oh my, I've got to do something, John is in trouble, and Mary has gotten into a terrible mess! I'd better act!" No! The Lord has already done all He is going to do. In fact, He did His work so well that when He rose up into the heavenlies, He sat down at the right hand of the Majesty on High. (See Hebrews 1:3.) Our high priest, Jesus Christ, is *sitting* on His throne. He has ceased from His labor. He has already procured our salvation with His blood and He has poured out on all who believe in Him all spiritual blessings that pertain to life and godliness. (See 2 Peter 1:3-4.)

The process of maturing in Christ Jesus is a process in which we learn more and more how to work outwardly what God has already placed in us inwardly. The process of spiritual maturity is learning how to live from the spiritual reality and blessings resident within us through the Holy Spirit.

Think for a moment about a baby in its mother's womb. That baby has every gene, every chromosome, every trait already built into it from the moment of conception. Likewise, God has placed the Holy Spirit in us to reveal the manifold spiritual characteristics, capabilities, and possibilities He has given for every aspect of our lives.

Furthermore, when we accept Jesus Christ as our Savior, we don't get just a few spiritual blessings. When Christ comes into us and we come into Christ, we are given *all* spiritual blessings. Paul wrote to the Corinthians:

> **E**ye hath not seen, nor ear heard, neither have entered into the heart of man, the things which God hath prepared for them that love him.
>
> 1 CORINTHIANS 2:9

When you are a newborn baby in Christ Jesus, you don't know all you have, who you are, and all that lies ahead for you. You don't know as a baby in the crib that your eyes are brown or that you will crawl around on the floor in a few months or that you will have the ability to talk and walk. In the same way, when you are a newborn babe in Christ, you don't yet know all the spiritual blessings that God has placed inside you. You don't know all that He has planned for you or all that He desires to do in you, through you, and for you.

Nonetheless, the fullness of spiritual blessings resides in you. Your work is to grow in your understanding of those blessings and then to seize them and live from them. Spiritual blessings are like a divine seed that has been planted firmly in the heart of faith. As time goes by, that seed is watered with the Word. Experiences in our lives break up the ground of our souls. Sometimes the Lord puts a little fertilizer on us. And for what purpose? So that the harvest that is already resident in the seed will begin to take root, grow, and burst forth!

When we go through a crisis time in our walk with the Lord, we don't need to go out and look for faith, grace, strength, or any other spiritual blessing. We have them already residing within us. What we need to learn in our walk with the Lord is how to access and walk in what is already there. We must become aware that there isn't another believer on this earth who possesses more of God than we possess right now. The difference is that some believers have learned how to access and walk in their spiritual blessings more than others.

I see many Christians today who go from this meeting to that meeting, from this person to that person, hoping that somebody has more of God's power. They are hoping that when that "more powerful" person prays for them, they will receive the miracle they desire. The Lord's plan for us is to get to the point where we don't need to turn to others to do what He desires to do directly within us. When we begin to understand how to walk in the reality of all that has been given to us, we will start laying hands on our own head...speaking peace to our own spirit...ministering to our own self ...commanding calm to our own nerves...and bringing peace to our own home.

God's desire is that we become aware of all the spiritual blessings He has already imparted to us, and then that we access those blessings and employ them for His glory. We are to use our spiritual blessings not only to get our own needs met, but to advance the purposes and plans of God on this earth, in this generation, whenever and wherever we have the opportunity.

If we could see the full harvest God has already imparted to us and planted within us, our minds and hearts could not contain the sight! Our eyes would be blinded by the glory of it, and our souls would burst with the thought of it. But one word of warning: The enemy also knows our potential. He is not ignorant of God's plan or God's gifts to us. He knows the harvest we can experience in our lives. He knows the potential of the blessings God has for us.

Therefore, when Satan comes at us in battles, troubles, and times of oppression, we need to recognize that he is not simply fighting us over where we are or what we are doing. The devil is fighting us over what has been deposited in us! He knows what can be released from us. He is intimidated by our destiny and is fighting to keep us from moving into and possessing the blessings that are ours.

> **E**ye hath not seen, nor ear heard, neither have entered into the heart of man, the things which God hath prepared for them that love him.
>
> But God hath revealed them unto us by his Spirit: for the Spirit searcheth all things, yea, the deep things of God.

1 CORINTHIANS 2:9-10

The vastness of the potential wealth that can be released from the Church is virtually incomprehensible to most believers. Most of us can't even begin to imagine all that God desires to do in us, through us, or for us. Nevertheless, God's desire is for us to allow the Holy Spirit to show it to us, and when we see it, to pursue it and refuse to let go until we have obtained it. When we do this, when we work outwardly all the spiritual blessings God has placed in us, we will touch a lost world with the saving, healing, delivering hand of Jesus.

3

CHOSEN

According as he hath chosen us in him before the foundation of the world, that we should be holy and without blame before him in love.

EPHESIANS 1:4

If not one human being on the face of the earth ever showed any love toward you or valued you in the slightest way, this verse in Ephesians shatters and dispels all that rejection and bondage by letting you know that *God chose you.* He chose you to be His beloved child before He even created the heavens and the earth. You are not an accident, a mistake, or an error. You were in Almighty God's heart and mind and plan for the universe long before the earth ever heard your first cry. Don't ever let anybody tell you and don't ever think or say that you are unloved or unwanted again!

There is no better way to appreciate the value of being chosen than to explore the definition of the word itself. It is the Greek word *exlegomai.*

Technically, the word simply means "to call out." The prefix *ex* means "out" or "out of" and *lego* means "to speak or lay out." We then could conclude that the Lord called us out of something. Yes, He did call us out of the kingdom of darkness into the kingdom of His dear Son, but there is more to discover in the word "chosen."

The grammar in the Greek language has a function for verbs called voice. The voice of the verb tells us about the relationship between the action of the verb and the subject. In this case, the voice teaches us that not only were we chosen, but we were chosen *for* the Lord *by* the Lord. His choosing us was not simply for an assignment in the kingdom, but we were chosen *for Him*. We are His treasure. Malachi 3:17 states that when God comes to make up His jewels, we shall be His. We are not just participants in the work of the kingdom, we are the treasure of God and for God.

The timing of this choosing is also very important. God made the decision, in the words of the *King James Version*, "from the foundation of the world." In the Greek text, "foundation" is the word *katabole*. This is such a special word picture! It means "to throw down or fling down." So then, we were chosen, called out, and picked before the Lord ever flung the stars in space, set the rivers in motion, or filled the nightingale's mouth with song. We were on God's mind from the very beginning of creation. We are not a last-minute change of mind or a reaction to a problem, but an integral part of God's initial design.

We are chosen by God to be His precious child.

We are created and hand-crafted by our Creator for a specific purpose.

We are wanted and valued by the Almighty King of the entire universe.

What a wonderful blessing it is — what a great source of emotional and spiritual wealth — to know that we are God's *chosen ones!*

We each know in the natural how special it is to be chosen. When we were children, we knew it was special to be chosen for a particular team, drama part, choir solo, or class project. When we started dating, we felt special when we were "chosen" to date someone we liked and admired. When we married, we were grateful that our spouse "chose" us to be their marriage partner and lover. When we gave birth to our children, we felt awe that God had "chosen" us and entrusted us with their precious lives. But there is nothing more awesome than to know that God chose us long before our birth to be in relationship with Him and to fulfill a part of His eternal plan.

God also chose you to be His child and to be a part of the body of Christ on the earth at precisely this time and in precisely the location where you find yourself. God does not randomly snatch people. You weren't just some piece of wood that fell down through a crack in the wall and God said, "Oh, all right, I'll go ahead and add this to the house." No! With great determination, deliberation, and design God said, "I want *you*. I'm going to use you for this particular job. I want your specific personality and your unique set of talents in this precise position at this significant time."

The Lord has crafted you and formed you and shaped you. He has molded you and made you. He knows your strengths, your weaknesses, your characteristics, and He has caused you to be a perfect fit and a perfect tool for a very precise and important role in His plan. You have been chosen just as the cedars of Lebanon were selected, one by one, for the building of Solomon's temple. Jesus said to His disciples, "You have not chosen Me, but I have chosen you." (See John 15:16.) The same is true for us today as His disciples on this earth.

What good news this is for us! No matter what might be right or wrong with us, or what we might like or dislike about ourselves, we must be all right with God, because He has chosen us for His work.

He is going to use us for the fulfillment of His plan. He is going to apply our unique personalities and abilities to a particular place and time in history.

Stop to think about this any time you feel tempted to start trying to be like another person. If you give up being who you are in order to become like somebody else, you are going to be duplicating a piece in the puzzle that God does not need two of! God needs for you to be *you*. He made you a precise way for a precise purpose and only *you as you* will do. When He called you, He wanted *you*. When He chose you, He wanted *you*. You are His treasure and His delight!

HOLY AND BLAMELESS

According as he hath chosen us in him before the foundation of the world, that we should be holy and without blame before him in love.

EPHESIANS 1:4

The first half of this verse deals with what has already been done, that before God ever created the universe, He chose us to be His precious children. The second half of the verse deals with what *will* be done as a result of our being chosen. Please hear this! We cannot be holy and without blame if we are not chosen!

The word "holy" and the "doctrine of holiness" based upon this word has been much misunderstood over time. Many theologically oriented rules and regulations have been tied to this word and this doctrine. There are complete religious organizations that identify themselves with the word "holy" or "holiness." To the religious Christian, "holy" often means a manner of dress, restriction of activities, and pride in the fact that certain sins have no effect on them. Unfortunately for them, "holy" does not mean those things!

The word "holy" is translated from the Greek word *hagios* and means "dedicated to God, sacred, reserved for God and His service." Holiness is not a Christian version of *Robert's Rules of Order*. While the Lord does want us to live in victory and moral integrity, He placed other specific teachings in His Word to cover those areas in our lives.

The word "holy" focuses our attention on our relationship to God. We are chosen or "called out" to be holy or "available for the exclusive use of God." We are dedicated to His purpose. A wonderful picture of this concept is found in the Old Testament tabernacle. When Moses received the charge to build the tabernacle, he was given specific pieces of furniture to construct and utensils to craft for the work that would take place there.

Some of those utensils were forks, spoons, basins, and fleshhooks. Please note that before they were dedicated to the temple, they were just ordinary forks, spoons, basins, and fleshhooks. But once they were consecrated to the tabernacle, they became holy forks, holy spoons, holy basins, and holy fleshhooks. From that point on, these utensils could no longer be used for just anyone, by anyone, because they were holy instruments. They could only be used in the temple ministries, available only for the exclusive use of God.

In the same way, believers in Jesus Christ are dedicated to and made holy for the service of our Lord. We are not just Fred and Helen; we are Holy Fred and Holy Helen. God's plan is that we walk before Him holy, completely consecrated and set apart for Him alone. So many people spend a lifetime wondering, "Why am I here? What purpose does God have for me?" God's purpose is that you be His holy vessel! When a believer goes through life with that truth always on their mind and embedded in their heart, they can never go far from God's will.

We are also to walk "without blame." In the Greek, blameless is *amomos*, which means "to be without flaw or without blemish." The word takes us back to the Old Testament sacrifices. When a lamb was offered to God in worship, its condition had to be flawless. A sickly, weak, or blemished lamb was disqualified as an acceptable offering to God.

Jesus Christ was our spotless and perfect sacrificial Lamb. He qualified for the position of our substitute by virtue of His blameless life. In Ephesians 1:4, Paul recognizes the sinless life of Jesus Christ and shows us that we are positionally holy — set apart for the exclusive use of God — and blameless — without flaw or blemish — in Christ.

Our experience, on the other hand, is not always quite as pristine! We are holy, which is being available for God's exclusive use. However, being holy takes both a mental commitment to pleasing God and a physical discipline to shun those things that offend Jesus Christ. Being blameless or without flaw in our daily experience can only be accomplished by submitting ourselves to the care and management of Jesus Christ. His Word, which continually cleanses us, and His Spirit, which enables us to resist our innate tendencies to fall and fail, are essential components for walking out the reality that we are blameless.

Ephesians 1:4 says we are, "holy and without blame *before him.*" The word "before" means to be continuously presenting ourselves to Jesus, to be constantly aware of His presence in our lives. Jesus told us that He would never leave us nor forsake us (see Hebrews 13:5), and that statement means so much more than just showing up when we get ourselves in terrible trouble. In essence, Jesus was saying, "I want you to be aware of something: You cannot go anywhere or do anything that I will not be there with you. You are always *before* Me."

Then the end of Ephesians 1:4 brings us to the capstone of the verse: in love. Now before I go on, I must tell you that there is great disagreement among Bible scholars and commentators about whether "in love" should be linked to verse 4 or verse 5, which begins "Having predestinated...." This controversy poses the question, "Are we holy and blameless before Him in love, or are we predestinated in love?" In my view, the exact answer will be known when we stand with Jesus and the apostle Paul in heaven. In the meantime, I see no heresy in enjoying God's love in both verses!

Without a doubt, the understanding that we have been chosen as God's treasure and for His purpose, that we are holy and set apart for His exclusive use, that we are found blameless in Christ Jesus, and that we are always in His presence must lead us to experience His incredible love. And certainly, without the experience of His grace-filled, life-transforming, unconditional love, it would be impossible for us to manifest a holy, blameless, walk of love toward others.

ACCORDING TO LOVE

No believer can live out Ephesians 1:4 in their own strength, ability, or desire. We must go back to the word "according" at the beginning of this verse to find the key to releasing the power of being holy and blameless before Him. "According" is the key that releases our destiny. It is translated from the Greek word, *kathos*, which means "even as, in conformity with the fact." I like to say that being in Christ places us "in the same dimension" as Jesus, conforming us to His image and declaring us holy and without blame before God.

In English, the word "according" is likened to a musical term: a chord, a harmonious blending together of notes. Our destiny is to be harmonious with what God has chosen for us. We must get in line — get in tune — with what God has planned for us to be and do. Any note that is dissonant or out of harmony with God's plan and purpose is a note that is going to jangle the nerves and cause distress to the body. It is going to create a noise, not a pleasant sound. It is going to disrupt, interfere, and be counterproductive to what God has planned for us and those whose lives we touch.

Our job is to recognize what God has planned for us and what is counter to His purposes, and then to choose only those things which are in harmony with God's plan. Have you ever sung harmony with another person? If you have, you know that the other person hits the first note and then you hit a note that sounds good with their note. Harmony only exists because there is first a melody. In our lives, God is the lead singer! He sings the melody line, and our role is to harmonize with Him. We must match His rhythm and His tempo. We must yield the "lead" to Him, saying, "Yes, I'll be Your holy vessel, totally submitted to whatever You desire to do in me and through me."

What we are describing here is nothing more than the act of being before Him in love. Isn't it interesting that the apostle Paul uses this musical analogy to describe love in another great epistle:

> **T**hough I speak with the tongues of men and of angels, and have not charity [love], I am become as sounding brass, or a tinkling cymbal.
> And though I have the gift of prophecy, and understand all mysteries, and all knowledge; and though I have all faith, so that I could remove mountains, and have not charity [love], I am nothing.

And though I bestow all my goods to feed the poor,
and though I give my body to be burned, and have not
charity [love], *it profiteth me nothing.*

1 CORINTHIANS 13:1-3

(BRACKETS MINE)

Our destiny can only be discovered and lived out as we walk in harmony with God, "according to" or "in the same dimension as" the powerful understanding that He has chosen us from time eternal. We are His precious vessel of honor. In Christ we are pure and without blemish. We are always conscious of His presence in our lives. In the knowledge of these truths, we will then sing in tune with His song of love toward us and through us to reach the world.

4

PREDESTINED

Having predestinated us unto the adoption of children by Jesus Christ to himself, according to the good pleasure of his will.

EPHESIANS 1:5

One of the greatest experiences a person will ever enjoy in life is being wanted by another person. To be needed, desired, and wanted is the supreme antidote for loneliness, depression, and low self-esteem. But, as precious as being wanted by another person is, it pales in comparison to being chosen by God.

BEFORE ENCIRCLED

In verse 4 we discussed the word *exlegomai*, to be called out or chosen. In verse 5 we have another word that gives us more details of God's sovereign choice, *prooridzo*, which is a compound word. *Pro* means "before" and *oridzo* means "encircle." So God encircled us before. He picked us out before we were born. The image the word portrays is like a person who is looking in a newspaper for a new home. He surveys the listings, looking for the perfect home which will give him the utmost pleasure and meet all his needs. After looking at all the houses being offered, he takes a pen and draws a circle around the one he wants. This is a crude example, but it does at least illustrate the fact that God specifically chose us for Himself.

God's choice was not a reaction to our overtures towards Him. He didn't choose us because of our actions, lifestyle, or pleadings. He chose us prior to our lives even beginning. He made the decision to be good to us without provocation, inducement, or cajoling. None of our weaknesses, failures, or personality flaws had any effect on His decision either. We had no influence on the decision, because we didn't exist yet, and we had no access to Him. God predestined us, or determined beforehand, that we would be His children.

In simple terms, to predestine or to "before encircle" is to predetermine. It means to have something in mind from the beginning. God is not making up His plan as He goes. His plan is set, established, in place. And He knows precisely what He needs at any given point to fulfill His plan.

I used to think that when movies were made, the director and actors started at the first scene and then worked their way through the movie scene by scene until they filmed the final scene of the movie. That's not how they do it, however. Many times, the last scene or a scene in the middle of the movie is shot first. Then the first scenes are shot so that they work into the later scenes. In many cases, the very beginning of the movie is the last part that is filmed. The director and actors can film in that way, because they are working with a script that gives them the whole story, beginning to end.

In a similar manner, the Lord has the full script for all time. He sees the ending from the beginning and every scene in between. The destiny of the world is determined. The outcome of history is fixed. That's one of the reasons God doesn't get hysterical about the things that cause us to get hysterical. When we run to Him and say, "I've been punched so hard! Don't You care? Couldn't You stop this fight?" the Lord responds to us calmly, saying, "The fight is fixed. I know who wins in the end."

The Lord has a master plan and a master strategy for every scene in your life. He sees how they all will fit together to tell a complete story that will bring glory to Him. What an awesome thought that we can be part of a scheme that is so grand and marvelous. Hell itself has not been able to thwart the plans of God. There is glory and victory ahead! And we are part of God's plan. We have been chosen from before the beginning of time for the role He has given us to play.

God's plan is fixed. It cannot and will not be edited or changed any more than God will change His own nature. He cannot be forced into a detour or into a delay. God is constant — the same yesterday, today, and forever. (See Hebrews 13:8.) You may ask, "But what about the sin of Adam and Eve in the Garden of Eden? Was that God's plan?"

Satan created a dilemma when Adam fell into sin. He took what God loved, which was man, and seduced him into partaking of what God hated, which was sin. Satan's purpose was to get God to work against Himself and to be in conflict with Himself by simultaneously loving man and hating sin. Do you see the problem that Satan created for God? For God to kill what He hated — sin — He would also have to kill what He loved — man.

God even had a strategy for dealing with this dilemma. In fact, He had a strategy in place before Satan created the dilemma! The Scriptures say that Jesus was the Lamb slain before the foundation of the world. (See Revelation 13:8.) In other words, before God created time or the universe, He devised the plan of redemption for man. Before man was created, in His omnipotence and fore-knowledge, God made provision for His will to be accomplished in every moment of history. That's why Satan has never been able to create a dilemma for God that God has not already outstrategized. There is nothing that the devil can throw at us and no obstacle he can put in our way that will alter the ultimate purpose of God for our lives. There is no way Satan can outmaneuver God!

We each must get to the place where we recognize that our God *acts* — He doesn't *react*. He is never on the defensive; He is always on the offensive. He never lets the enemy throw the first punch and then say, "Oh, what am I going to do to respond to that?" No! God acts sovereignly. Nothing that the enemy does can abort what God has decreed, and no action of the enemy can thwart His plan.

ADOPTED CHILDREN
ARE *WANTED* CHILDREN

Having predestinated us into the adoption of children by Jesus Christ to himself, according to the good pleasure of his will.

EPHESIANS 1:5

When God "before encircled" us, He had something very specific in mind. He was adopting us. "Adoption" is the Greek word *huiothesiah*, from *huios* (son) and *tithemi* (to place), "to place as a son." *Huios* (pronounced wee-os) is very significant here. There are two primary words for children: *teknia* and *huios*. *Teknia* represents children who are teenagers and younger. *Huios* represents children who are full-grown. Literally, this verse of Scripture is telling us that God adopted us as full-grown adults!

In our culture, adoption focuses on very small children and babies. The thought is to avoid having personality conflicts and to look as normal as possible by adopting a young child or infant. Their personalities are not yet formed and it looks like the couple had the child through childbirth if they are little. Therefore, adopting babies and very small children is preferred. However, in the time in which Paul wrote, adoption was usually restricted to people of means. When a person had great wealth but no heir, they would look for a full-grown man who possessed the qualities they wanted to be remembered by after they were dead. They would adopt, knowing their name would be well represented in the future.

Older children and adults are not easily adopted, no matter what time it is, because they are set in their ways, personality, and character. However, biblical adoption takes advantage of this fact to express the love of God, for God adopted us knowing who we were and how we were. God didn't choose to adopt us because we were qualified for the assignment. He chose the failing, incompetent, and poorly trained. All of those flaws did not hinder or deter Him from choosing us. God's adopting us gave us value and significance.

> *For ye see your calling, brethren, how that not many wise men after the flesh, not many mighty, not many noble, are called.*
>
> 1 CORINTHIANS 1:26

Adoption blesses us because it assures us God wanted us regardless of our faults, failings, and weaknesses. He predestined us, or picked us out and encircled us by Himself and for Himself to adopt, to be His child. No matter what our natural abilities or character or attitude, He chose us just as we were.

Today, when a couple is going to have a child, they speculate about what the child will be like and who the child will be. Our modern technology has stolen some of the mystique of child-bearing by allowing us to know the sex of the child before they are born. But not even technology can predict with accuracy what the child will be like. We cannot know for certain whether they will be bright or challenged, articulate or mute, passionate or sedate. The best a couple can hope for is a healthy child who has a teachable spirit.

Adoption, on the other hand, is not such a mystery. When a family adopts a child, they know exactly what their child looks like and what their interests are. They are fully aware of the personality traits and quirks which constitute their adopted child's life. Likewise, when a child is adopted, they know that their adopting parents want them for who they are and what they are. Their new parents are fully aware of their faults, failings, strengths, and passions.

The wonderful thing about adoption is that nobody ever adopted a child they didn't want. Some people give birth to babies they don't want, but nobody *adopts* a baby they don't want. God has wanted you since before the world was created. The relationship He has desired for you for countless ages past is that you be His adopted child. Through the ages, He arranged the details of His plan in order to bring you to the point where you would accept Jesus Christ as your Savior and be a part of His family.

Many people think they got saved because one morning they awoke and they decided to get saved.

Certainly there comes a point where we must say "yes" to what God has already said "yes" to, but the greater reality is this: You are saved because it was the good pleasure of *His* will to save you. God wanted you. He drew you with cords of love.

HIS GOOD PLEASURE

Having predestinated us unto the adoption of children by Jesus Christ to himself, according to the good pleasure of his will.

EPHESIANS 1:5

Nothing defeats the good effects and satisfaction of something done for us like the discovery that it was done with a bad attitude. When we learn that someone did something for us because they were forced to, or they did it grumbling through the whole process, we take no pleasure in what they did for us. There is no joy in this kind of "good deed," and we wish they would have never got involved with us.

Paul is assuring us that God adopted us "according to the pleasure of his will." If God had not taken pleasure in us, our salvation would have become nothing more than a mandatory rescue mission. We would still have been delivered, but no intimate relationship with our Deliverer would have occurred. There was great potential for God to take this route. We were an undone people who had repeatedly rejected His offers of love. Our rebellion had no effect, however, on His commitment to save us. The decision had already been made in eternity past for one reason only: it *pleased* Him.

The Greek word for "will" used here is *thelema*, "a desire which proceeds from one's heart or emotions." I cannot imagine what it is about us that would cause God to desire us and to derive pleasure from just thinking about being good to us. He was pleased about our being saved long before He actually saved us! Before we arrived on the scene, God the Director knew exactly who was going to play what part in His extravaganza of life on earth.

An actress might go to an audition thinking that she is trying out for a part in a play. And when she gets that part she may think that she got it totally on her own merits and acting skill. What a surprise it is for her to learn later that the director knew precisely who and what he was looking for. He knew long before the auditions took place what kind of person it would take to play the part. He knew the personality, look, and characteristics required. She didn't win the part — she was pre-selected for the part. She simply pursued and said "yes" to the part that had already been given to her.

God's will for us is intimately born from the joy He takes in us. He has predestined us to be His child, the apple of His eye, and He has done this because it was the desire of His heart and because it gave Him the utmost pleasure.

THE DIVINE ARCHITECT

A verse of Scripture that always used to blow my mind is Psalm 127:1:

> Except the Lord build the house, they labour in vain that build it.

I thought, *If God has already built the house, why is anybody laboring to build it and how could it be in vain?* Then one day I began to understand that God is not the carpenter. He's the *architect*. He builds by design, and then we, like carpenters, manifest in time and space what God has designed in eternity. An architect lays out on paper all of the specs and weights and dimensions, and then he stands back and appraises his plan. He can "see" that plan fully realized. He envisions all that He has drawn on paper in the three-dimensional reality in his mind, including the landscaping!

All of the blueprints for a building are in place before any construction begins. A building doesn't get built to a certain point and then the construction is stopped so the architect can work on the plumbing layout or the electrical plan. All of the plans are in place before the first shovelful of dirt is moved.

God's plan has been in place for all time and before time. God's blueprints are exact, precise, and complete. They give all the details necessary for the total project, start to finish. And His master blueprint includes a specific blueprint precisely for you and me. God sees the fullness of who we can be, right down to the minutest detail. His plan for us is flawless and better than any plan we could ever conceive for ourselves.

When we try to build a plan for ourselves that is different from God's perfect plan, we labor in vain. Our efforts are futile. They count for nothing. On the other hand, when we yield to God's plan and allow Him to build His plan by the power of the Holy Spirit at work in us, we move toward perfection and wholeness.

When we understand and accept our position as believers in Jesus Christ — that God has predestined us to be His children and this gives Him the greatest pleasure — our only obligation is to choose what God has chosen for us. We must say "yes" to all that He has designed — our purpose, our relationship with Him and other people, our destiny, our ministry. We must choose to develop all that He has put in us so that we can use what He has put into us for His purposes.

> *Study to show thyself approved unto God, a workman that needeth not to be ashamed, rightly dividing the word of truth.*
>
> 2 TIMOTHY 2:15

We are to be workmen who have developed all of our capabilities, talents, and spiritual assets. When the time comes to employ those talents for God's purposes, we can perform with excellence and the Holy Spirit will empower us, strengthen us, guide us, and help us. Then a most remarkable miracle occurs! Not only is God abundantly pleased with us, but we find ourselves completely overwhelmed by the joy and pleasure of being His child and fulfilling His plan.

5

BELOVED

To the praise of the glory of his grace, wherein he hath made us accepted in the beloved.

EPHESIANS 1:6

I used to spend a great deal of my time and energy trying to be accepted by other people. I wanted them to like me, respect me, admire me, and desire to have me around. But once I realized and understood the full weight of the fact that I was accepted in the Beloved of God, I no longer felt any need to walk into a room and ask the crowd to accept me. It ceased to be significant to me what others thought about me or whether I was accepted into certain cliques. A person who comprehends that they are accepted in the Beloved is a person who has all the acceptance they will ever need.

However, please do not misunderstand what I am saying here. I did not become indifferent, uncaring, and unmoved by people. This is not what happens when we are set free from the opinions of others by our acceptance in the Beloved! On the contrary, I became more concerned, more caring, and deeply moved by other people's needs, *because my own needs were being met by God.*

Once I grasped the depth and breadth of God's acceptance of me, all of my motivation and drive turned to pleasing Him alone. And when your every thought is consumed with pleasing God and carrying out His agenda, you find very quickly that He is only interested in touching other people in the same way He touched you. So rather than being desperate for another person's love and good opinion, I became desperate for them to know God and to be accepted in the Beloved also.

GRACE IS THE PLACE

In the original Greek text, the word for "accepted" is *charitoo*, which is derived from *charis*, the word for grace. *Charitoo* gives a much vaster meaning to acceptance! God does not merely tolerate our presence, but He has *graced* us. He has given us something we could not possibly give ourselves. He has graced us with His most cherished and loved possession: Jesus Christ. He has placed us in the Beloved, in Christ.

The Greek word for "Beloved" is *agapao*. Most believers are very familiar with the word from which *agapao* is derived, *agape*. Where *agape* is the love of God expressed, *agapao* is the object of His love, someone who gives Him eternal joy. So God has graced us by placing us in Christ, His Beloved, and in Christ we are now the object of His love and give Him eternal joy. We are now free to breathe in and breathe out His unconditional love. He has bestowed His honor upon us and crowns us with His glory.

Also, notice that Ephesians 1:6 says we *have* been accepted. Again, our acceptance is in the past tense, something God decided before time existed. We don't have to hope we're accepted, work to be accepted, or wonder if we'll ever be accepted. We are already accepted! We've got a membership card, a pass, and an ID badge that say, "Accepted in the Beloved." Why? Because for eternity God has loved and always will love Jesus, and we are in Him. We are in the place of grace!

It's important for us to recognize that we are accepted not on the basis of who we are, but on the basis of our position in Christ Jesus. This is the *charitoo* or grace of being in the Beloved. God is not persuaded to accept us by anything we do, say, accomplish, earn, or "work up" in ourselves. We aren't accepted on the basis of the resume we compile or the track record we achieve. We are accepted totally because we have received Jesus as our Lord and Savior and are now in Christ. We have believed that Jesus is the Son of God, who was crucified on our behalf, resurrected for our hope, and ascended to heaven where He is our high priest and mediator. We are accepted because we are in relationship with God through Jesus Christ's shed blood — no other reason.

TRANSFORMING GRACE

The fact that God accepted me in the Beloved transformed my prayer life. Once I realized that I already had a pass directly into the throne room of God and He wanted me to be there, I no longer tried to talk God into hearing me. I could come boldly before Him at two o'clock in the morning, and I wasn't going to awaken Him, disturb Him, or interrupt Him. I could call on Him and know immediately that I was received with love and heard with concern. I realized that God was hearing me whether I screamed or whispered, regardless of the time or day, and no matter where I was or what I was doing. God was going to hear me and answer me just as He heard Jesus and answered Him, because I was graced to be in Christ. I was accepted in the Beloved.

When you grasp the fact that you are accepted in the Beloved and that you have the *full* acceptance of God, all of your low self-esteem is going to be healed. All of your reluctance to come to God with your sins and your needs is going to vanish. All of your shyness toward Him is going to disappear. You are in His Beloved. Nothing and nobody can ever change that fact.

> **T**here is therefore now no condemnation to them which are in Christ Jesus, who walk not after the flesh, but after the Spirit.
>
> ROMANS 8:1

We cannot shut off, stop, or in any way diminish God's flow of love toward us. No matter what we do, we cannot cause God to stop loving us.

Nothing can move us from the position of being loved by God.

Nothing can change the way God feels about us.

Nothing can alter the fact that God is going to continue to love us no matter what we do or say.

Receiving God's love heals us on the inside. It causes a person's self-esteem to be built up and emotional hurts to be soothed.

Receiving God's love allows us to feel value, worth, and dignity.

Receiving God's love allows us to respect ourselves.

Receiving God's love motivates us to discipline ourselves.

Receiving God's love gives us the capacity to return His love, love ourselves, and love others.

We are not only chosen by God, but we are eternally, tenderly, unconditionally, and infinitely loved by God. There is no greater blessing, no greater assurance!

THE GLORY OF HIS GRACE

To the praise of the glory of his grace, wherein he hath made us accepted in the beloved.

EPHESIANS 1:6

The word "wherein" points us to why we have been accepted in the Beloved: the glory of God's grace. Yes, we made the decision to receive Jesus as Lord and Savior, but the opportunity was there for us not because we were good enough, but because God was good enough to offer it to us. "Wherein" emphatically tells us that it is God's grace that makes us accepted in the Beloved.

This grace is not just a thin, whimsical, just-enough grace. God's grace is glorious and beyond human understanding. The word "glory" expresses all the attributes of God's grace: excellence in character, exceeding wisdom, unfathomable love, resplendent honor and esteem, and a brilliant countenance which reflects the essence and power of eternal life. God's grace is glorious, and we should praise Him continuously for it!

We are transformed by our position in Christ Jesus because we come face to face with the living reality of God's glorious grace toward us. In this most privileged position, we must never cease to humbly offer our praise of thanksgiving and awe to God, whose very nature made us accepted in the Beloved.

6

REDEEMED AND FORGIVEN

In whom we have redemption through his blood, the forgiveness of sins, according to the riches of his grace.

EPHESIANS 1:7

Most people I know, including believers, are more concerned about their "current condition" than their "eternal position." Let me declare today: It's time we quit worrying about our *condition* and started focusing on our *position*, because our condition will never change until we understand our position. Any condition of our life is temporal. Conditions change. They come and go. Our position, on the other hand, is eternal. It never diminishes, it never changes, and it cannot be destroyed. And what a position we have! Our position in Christ Jesus is first and foremost that we are redeemed and forgiven.

Redemption literally means "payment of ransom." Now "ransom" does not mean a figure in a black ski mask comes into your bedroom at two in the morning, snatches you, and leaves a note for your parents that he will kill you if they don't give him a million dollars by high noon the next day. Adam was not kidnapped in the Garden of Eden. He knowingly and willfully disobeyed God's directive and ate of the tree of the knowledge of good and evil.

Our redemption, or payment of ransom, pictures God as the righteous judge who must hold us in prison, under a sentence of eternal death and damnation, because of our sin. But when He sees the blood of Jesus, which symbolizes the giving of Jesus' pure and sinless life, God is satisfied that the ransom for sin has been paid. When we accept Jesus as Lord and Savior, our prison door swings open and we are free!

For all have sinned, and come short of the glory of God.

ROMANS 3:23

The only way we could be free from the inevitable execution of our eternal death sentence was that a ransom would be paid for us. The problem was, no matter how hard we tried or how dedicated we were to settling our account, we could not in five lifetimes pay this debt. Only Jesus could satisfy the debt against us because He was the only one in all of human history who could offer a life completely free from sin. His blood symbolized His death for

all mankind. Jesus offered Himself as a substitute
for us.

> **F**orasmuch as ye know that ye were not redeemed
> with corruptible things, as silver and gold...;
> But with the precious blood of Christ, as of a lamb
> without blemish and without spot.
>
> 1 PETER 1:18-19

When God saw Jesus' precious blood, His wrath
upon the sin of man was appeased, our debt was
paid, and our release was secured. When we receive
Jesus as our Lord and Savior, we are free to enjoy
the blessings of God and fellowship with Him. In
fact, the payment of our debt was what Jesus had in
mind at Calvary when He said "Tetelestai." The King
James Version translates that word as, "It is finished,"
but the more accurate translation is, "Paid in full."
Jesus paid in full forever our debt to God — and God
was fully satisfied. We are no longer condemned
prisoners awaiting our execution because God's
judgment and wrath upon our sin have been satisfied through the shedding of Jesus' blood.

NEW POSITION MEANS
NEW CONDITION

Our incarceration was positional, but it
manifested in our condition. Before we believed in

Jesus we were slaves to sin. Before Jesus Christ purchased our redemption, we couldn't help but sin. It was our very nature to sin. Whatever the devil tempted us to do, we usually did it and didn't think anything about it. Then Jesus snatched us off the slave table. He took us out of the slave auction and said, "Sin, never again will you have control over them!" He looked at us and said, "You are free! You no longer need to sin. You can choose to walk boldly in the Spirit and to do what is holy, blameless, and loving before God."

It is not enough for an emancipation proclamation of redemption to be issued if the slaves don't know about it! And the master of slaves is the last person in the world who wants to tell them that an emancipation proclamation has been issued. If you don't know you are free, you'll remain in bondage in your mind, and where the mind goes, so goes your life. That's why the devil's main ministry is to tell you and convince you that you do not have redemption.

If you don't know Ephesians 1:7, which plainly tells you that you have redemption through Jesus' blood, then you'll continue to do whatever your slave master tells you. You have no awareness or understanding that you can do anything other than what he says. You'll be like a bird that remains in a cage even though the door to the cage has been blown open by the power of Almighty God.

I'm here to tell you today that you are FREE! Jesus has redeemed you from the need to remain bound to your old sins. You no longer have to sin! You may say, "Are you saying that a believer doesn't sin or that a believer never sins?" No — I'm saying a believer doesn't *have* to sin.

> **M**y little children, these things write I unto you, that ye sin not. And if any man sin, we have an advocate with the Father, Jesus Christ the righteous.
>
> 1 JOHN 2:1

Some believers do sin, but they don't have to. They can choose not to. Sin doesn't have to be part of the believer's life. And if we do sin, 1 John 1:9 tells us we must go quickly to the Father to confess it, and He will erase it and cleanse us from all unrighteousness. We can live free of sin.

What is dominating you right now? Are you aware that you can be free of that domination?

Are you in bondage to sexual sins and desires you can't control?

Are you locked into a way of thinking that leads you into the darkness of depression?

Are you ensnared with hate for certain people and always angry in certain situations?

Hear me! Jesus has *redeemed* you from that. You don't need to be in bondage any longer. You don't need to listen to the old slave master of your soul another second. You have been bought out of the marketplace of sin, and the devil and your flesh no longer have a right to speak to your life, control you, or dominate you. You have the full right to use the name of Jesus to rebuke every depression, fear, carnal desire, and humanistic thought that attempts to bind you, inhibit you, or keep you from freedom to love and worship God. Jesus holds the papers that say, "Paid in full!"

Any time the devil says to you, "That's just your nature...that's just the way you are...that's the way God made you...that's normal human behavior" — you can count on two things being true. First, the behavior the devil is calling normal, acceptable, or inevitable is anything but normal, acceptable, or inevitable for the believer. It may be normal for the sinner who hasn't received Jesus Christ as Savior, but it isn't normal for the believer.

> **K**now ye not that the unrighteous shall not inherit the kingdom of God? Be not deceived: neither fornicators, nor idolaters, nor adulterers, nor effeminate, nor abusers of themselves with mankind,
> Nor thieves, nor covetous, nor drunkards, nor revilers, nor extortioners, shall inherit the kingdom of God.

And such were some of you: but ye are washed, but ye are sanctified, but ye are justified in the name of the Lord Jesus, and by the Spirit of our God.

1 CORINTHIANS 6:9-11

Notice that word "were." Believers are no longer what they once *were*. We have been washed, sanctified, and justified by the shed blood of Jesus and now have the sweet but strong presence of the Holy Spirit in our lives. What was once normal is no longer normal. Only God's will and ways are normal.

Second, the devil is a liar and he cannot tell the truth about you or about what is true in God's eyes. Whatever the devil says to you about you isn't going to be the truth. When he tries to tell you who you are and who you aren't, tell him who he is — a liar and the father of all lies. (See John 8:44.)

You can count on the fact that Jesus came to tell you the opposite of anything the devil tells you. Jesus says to you, "Here's My nature. That's the nature God has for you. Live in it. You don't need to live the way you lived before. You don't need to do what you did before. You can be free of those old habits, attitudes, and lusts. You can be free of those old fears, doubts, and negative thoughts. I came to give you life and to give it to you fully and abundantly." (See John 10:10.)

To the person who has been a slave, there is nothing more valuable — no mark of wealth that is more meaningful or important — than being set free. Freedom is the prize of all people, everywhere, in all ages. It is one of the greatest and most valuable "possessions" any person can have.

The truly wealthy are those who possess the riches of heaven, and one of those riches is redemption, which frees us from the wrath of God upon our sin. Because Jesus gave His life and our debt of sin was paid, God is no longer our enemy. When we come into Christ and are born again, the reality of redemption changes our entire perspective on life. We now begin to comprehend the freedoms our new position yields: to be God's child, to know Him, to commune with Him, to worship Him, and to carry out His marvelous and miraculous plan for our lives — totally free from the shackles of sin.

To be free from sin means that we are able to accept and act upon the reality that we are chosen and loved.

To be free from sin means that we have a potential for spiritual growth and learning.

To be free from sin means that all of the bondages of the flesh that have kept us limited and immobile are removed. Our spirits are free to soar, to dream

God's dreams, to enter into God's purposes, and to claim God's promises.

A NEW START

In whom we have redemption through his blood, the forgiveness of sins, according to the riches of his grace.

EPHESIANS 1:7

In Jesus, we have redemption through His precious blood. The ransom for our debt of sin has been paid in full and God is satisfied. In light of this incredible and nearly incomprehensible truth, I have just declared to you that you no longer need to be a slave to sin. Did you wonder how I could say that? It is because you also have *forgiveness* of sins. Forgiveness is intimately related to and a product of redemption.

In the original text, the word for "forgiveness" is *aphesis*. This means more than a dismissal of accountability. *Aphesis* is the *cancellation* of an obligation, punishment, or guilt. The penalty for your sin is gone, washed away by the blood of Jesus! Not only have you been redeemed from slavery to sin, but all of your sins have been completely erased. Your evil past has been completely obliterated and washed away by Jesus Christ, and every sin you commit from the day you were born again, once repented of, is also washed away.

>**A**s far as the east is from the west, so far hath he removed our transgressions from us.
>
>PSALM 103:12

When the Lord forgives, He chooses also to forget.

>**I** will forgive their iniquity, and I will remember their sin no more.
>
>JEREMIAH 31:34

>**I** will be merciful to their unrighteousness, and their sins and their iniquities will I remember no more.
>
>HEBREWS 8:12

Notice that word "will." The Bible doesn't say that God is forgetful or that He can't remember. It says God chooses not to remember. He *wills* to forget. There are many believers today who need to *will* to forget their sins once they have confessed them to God and have been forgiven of them. They need to accept the fullness of the forgiveness God offers them and to choose not to remember their sins also.

The more we recall our sins and rehearse them, the more we reinforce those terrible memories in our minds. The more we think about our past sins and moan and groan over them, the more we keep the knowledge of them alive in our soul. Then, when we hold our sin as a thought in our thought bank, it is more likely that we are going to act on that thought.

Don't keep a remembrance of your sin around like a "pet memory." If sin is a "pet," it is a viper! It kills. The memory of sin is a deadly force. When sin is allowed to lie dormant in our minds and hearts, it is still alive. We are allowing it to have power over us. Just as no man can ever fully predict when a live but dormant volcano is going to erupt, so we are never able to predict when a live but dormant sin will rise up and come roaring out of our minds, turning our words to hot coals and our behavior to a blaze of destruction. Only by forgiving ourselves and forgetting our sin can we truly kill its influence and impact on us.

Choose to forget what God has forgiven and forgotten!

If someone comes to you and says, "Did you ever...?" answer that person, "I don't remember. If I did that, God forgave me for it and the Bible says He forgot about it. If He forgave me and forgot about it, there is no reason for me to remember it." Shame is not a blessing! It is a weight Jesus carried for you on the cross. Therefore, the weight of your past sins is a weight you should set down and walk away from!

THE RICHES OF GOD'S GRACE

The phrase "riches of his grace" expresses the value of God's unmerited favor toward us. The word "riches" by itself is very attractive. It could mean wealth or extreme value, or it could mean those things that are precious to a person or group of people. However, in this passage the significance of the word "riches" is that it means both "abundant" *and* "precious."

Now, "abundant" and "precious" aren't always compatible concepts. For example, a diamond is precious because it is not found in abundance. "Abundance" means a lot of something; "precious" means rare or unique. What makes God's grace precious is that the purchase price for our redemption is the unique blood of Jesus shed at Calvary.

Jesus' blood and only His blood qualified to purchase our redemption. It wasn't the blood itself, but the fact that His blood was absolutely free from sin and therefore pure and perfect. His pure and perfect blood is what 1 Peter 1:19 calls "precious blood." That precious blood is what was freely and liberally spent to redeem us. His precious blood is the substance of the riches of His grace.

However, Paul declares that the grace of God we enjoy is both precious *and* abundant. The abundant part of riches suggests the manner in which those riches are distributed to us. We do not receive a sampling of His grace, a smidgen of His grace, a whiff of His grace, or a little dab of His grace. NO! He lavishes His grace on us! The picture is of a rich person who goes on a buying binge or splurge. In other words, God indulges Himself in the luxury of pouring His grace upon our lives.

Now we face another dispute among the theologians. Some believe "the riches of his grace" belongs with Ephesians 1:7: "the forgiveness of sins, according to the riches of his grace," others argue that it must be attached to Ephesians 1:8: "According to the riches of his grace; wherein he hath abounded toward us in all wisdom and prudence." Either way, we must stand dumbfounded and awestruck at the riches of God's grace!

For verse 7, we are humbled and brought to our knees that our forgiveness is not based upon making amends or doing good works. Our forgiveness is based solely on the riches of God's grace. God chooses to forgive us because His grace is both exceedingly abundant and precious beyond imagination. He chooses to see us as completely pure, pure beyond our wildest dreams, because we are in Christ Jesus. Paul wrote to the Ephesians very directly about this matter.

> **F**or by grace are ye saved through faith; and that
> not of yourselves: it is the gift of God:
> Not of works, lest any man should boast.
>
> EPHESIANS 2:8-9

You can't earn forgiveness.

You can't buy it.

You can't achieve it.

You can't accomplish it.

You can't become so good that you deserve it.

God chooses to grace us with forgiveness not because we are so worthy and wonderful, but because Jesus made us worthy and wonderful by the shedding of His blood. The only thing that is required of us to receive forgiveness is for us to admit that we need it and to ask Him for it. Again, John wrote, "If we confess our sins, he is faithful and just to forgive us our sins, and to cleanse us from all unrighteousness" (1 John 1:9).

When we confess our sins, which is to admit our sins, God forgives us. He does so for the sake of Jesus. He looks upon the shed blood of Jesus and says, "Because of what My Son did for you on the cross, and because you are accepting what My Son did for you, I forgive you." Forgiveness is never about what we have done — it is always about what Jesus has done!

Forgiveness is a grace gift from God, and there is no genuine forgiveness apart from Him. Many people in the world today are trying to forgive themselves for horrible sins. They are looking into mirrors and saying to themselves, "I'm okay. I'm good. I'm just fine the way I am." Apart from Christ, they are trying to forgive what they have no authority or power to forgive. Jesus said that He had authority to forgive sin, and He proved it by healing the physical body. (See Mark 2:10 and Matthew 9:6.) Then Jesus passed His authority to us.

> *Then said Jesus to them again, Peace be unto you: as my Father hath sent me, even so send I you.*
>
> *And when he had said this, he breathed on them, and saith unto them, Receive ye the Holy Ghost:*
>
> *Whose soever sins ye remit, they are remitted unto them; and whose soever sins ye retain, they are retained.*
>
> JOHN 20:21-23

Out of the unfathomable riches of God's grace, the limitless and precious grace of God, we are swept away in the tide of His ocean of mercy and find ourselves going beyond our own redemption to extend God's grace to others. We experience a new and tantalizing miracle. As God forgives us and we receive His forgiveness, we are able to forgive ourselves and others.

For thou, Lord, art good, and ready to forgive; and plenteous in mercy unto all Them who call upon thee.

PSALM 86:5

How many people in the world — and the Church is no exception — are walking in overwhelming shame and guilt because they cannot forgive themselves, or debilitating anger and frustration because they cannot forgive those who offended and hurt them? I believe many, and possibly most, of the world's problems and struggles would disappear if the life-transforming truths of redemption and forgiveness were understood by believers and lived before the world. The life of God courses freely through the vessel who knows and fully comprehends that they are redeemed and forgiven.

SEALED

Wherein he hath abounded toward us in all wisdom and prudence;

Having made known unto us the mystery of his will, according to his good pleasure which he hath purposed in himself:

That in the dispensation of the fulness of times he might gather together in one all things in Christ, both which are in heaven, and which are on earth; even in him.

EPHESIANS 1:8-10

These verses of Scripture are interconnected and intimately linked to one another as well as to both the verses that precede and follow them. For example, after exploring "the riches of his grace" in Ephesians 1:7, we can begin to comprehend the eternal, Almighty God abounding toward us in all His wisdom and prudence. The apostle Paul probably used the colorful and descriptive term "abounding" because it depicts an excessively extravagant gesture that reflects the incredible riches of God's grace.

We are then moved to the next level of revelation: God's wisdom and prudence are lavished upon us. But we cannot stop there, because wisdom and prudence impact directly and describe in detail the "mystery of his will." Next we are immediately confronted again that all this is "according to his good pleasure which he hath purposed in himself," and has nothing at all to do with us, our goodness or good deeds. This passage speaks solely of the goodness of our God.

Verse 9 brings us to the brink of spiritual overload when we see that God is making known "the mystery of his will...that in the dispensation of the fulness of times he might gather together in one all things in Christ, both which are in heaven, and which are on earth." This verse epitomizes the literal theme of chapter 1 of Ephesians: Look what God has done for you and given to you! It is precious. It is gracious. It is awesome and magnificent and beyond description. It was determined in eternity past, based solely on God's grace and goodness, and delivered to you now.

In verse 8, wisdom and prudence show us *how* God delivered redemption to us. Wisdom is the Greek word *sophia*, a marvelous word! It not only speaks of skill and discernment, but also of infinite goodness and grace. Wisdom is then coupled with prudence, *phronesis* in the Greek, which means "the most effective way to attain the desired end." As glorious as the riches of God's grace are, the *method* of how God brought all of this into being is equally glorious. With incredible skill and goodness He used the most beneficial and effective path to forge our redemption.

A tremendous illustration of this point can be found in the state of Nevada, USA. There we find a monument to the creative genius of man called the Hoover Dam. It is so big, you can see it from an airplane five miles above the ground. When you visit the Hoover Dam, the tour guide first allows you to gaze upon this great marvel that restrains and controls the flow of trillions of tons of water. It is awesome to behold. After you take in all of the dam's splendor, the guide then takes you to a presentation room, where you view a documentary about the construction of the dam.

People who watch the movie are spellbound as they see and hear just how the dam was built. For you see, as majestic as the Hoover Dam is in its final state, the way they built it is just as superb and awe-inspiring. Likewise, in verse 8 Paul says that as precious as our redemption is, God has chosen to reveal not only the fact that we are redeemed, but the manner in which we were redeemed. We are incited to worship God not only because of what He did for us, but *how* He did it.

Prudence is applying wisdom to any circumstance or situation. Prudence is the outworking of wisdom. It is wisdom appropriated and applied to the practical situations and circumstances of life. God abounds toward us in both wisdom and demonstration or application. There is no problem He cannot solve, no situation with which He cannot deal.

Wisdom and prudence lie at the heart of all of our human capabilities, capacities, and abilities. It is wonderful to possess great physical strength, but we must know when and how to use it to be effective in the kingdom of God. Prudence takes wisdom and employs knowledge as God desires, developing intellectual capacity but also walking in good sense. Wisdom and prudence harvest and develop talent for God's glory and purposes.

THE MYSTERY OF GOD'S WILL

Having made known unto us the mystery of his will, according to his good pleasure which he hath purposed in himself:

That in the dispensation of the fulness of times he might gather together in one all things in Christ, both which are in heaven, and which are on earth; even in him.

EPHESIANS 1:9-10

As we examine this passage, we see that verse 10 describes the mystery of God's will mentioned in verse 9. The mystery referred to here is that Jesus Christ is the reconciler. At the perfect time, as God purposed in Himself from before the foundation of the world, all things in heaven and earth will one be in Christ. The mystery that is now being revealed to us is this: Jesus Christ is the place of reconciliation.

Now the word "dispensation" must not be confused with the Christian doctrine that there are specific time periods in which God works in certain ways: the Dispensation of Grace, the Dispensation of Human Government, etc. The word translated dispensation is *oikonomia*, which technically means "house rule or law." Its applied meaning is "administration, management, or stewardship."

It pleased God to share with us the mystery, the concealed details of His will, which were before this time unavailable to us. The mystery of His will essentially is Jesus Christ reconciling God to man. The specifics of the "mystery of his will" are how Jesus administrates or *dispenses* the will of God as the reconciler.

The fullness of times refers to the moment in time when the work of Jesus Christ is fully accomplished. In that work, Jesus reconciles the estranged parties, God and sinful man. The reconciliation spoken of here is both comprehensive and powerful. God had a solution to the problem of sin all along, but He didn't reveal His solution — Jesus Christ — until the fullness of times.

What is the ultimate truth we can know about God's will? "That in the dispensation of the fulness of times he might gather together in one all things in Christ, both which are in heaven, and which are on earth; even in him!" The mystery of God's will is not His will concerning our personal lives, but His will for the future of all mankind. His will for us is always embedded in that larger and more comprehensive will. We need to know God's master plan before we can fully comprehend what our part of that plan may be. Ephesians 1:10 is the beginning of Paul's explanation of the "big picture."

GOD'S INHERITANCE

In whom [Christ Jesus] *also we have obtained an inheritance, being predestinated according to the purpose of him who worketh all things after the counsel of his own will.*

EPHESIANS 1:11

A careful study of "obtained an inheritance" reveals that the Greek language reads quite differently from the *King James* translation. Literally, as we are in

Christ, we have not "obtained an inheritance," but we have been *made* an inheritance, "being predestinated [before encircled] according to the purpose of him [God the Father]." At this point, our hands and hearts must rise up to worship the God who has repeatedly told us and revealed to us that we are His precious chosen ones. At the death of His Son, God marked us as His personal inheritance!

Verse 11 then goes on to say that our great God "worketh all things after the counsel of his own will." Every step of the way, every day, and in countless ways, God is working all things in our lives toward the glorious future He has planned for us. He is continually working *all* things — not some things, not a few things, but *all* things — to the point where we will know, receive, and live within the fullness of all He has for us in Christ Jesus.

What does it mean for God to "work" all things? It means He is constantly manipulating, moving, maneuvering, and arranging all things according to His purposes. Things don't happen at random in our lives. They don't happen because of coincidence. God is at work, bringing about His purposes. If we are experiencing tribulation, we must glory in it! Tribulation works patience, and patience, experience, and experience, hope, and hope dispels all shame. (See Romans 5:3-5.) God is in the process of taking the worst things imaginable and turning them for great good in our lives. Circumstances may not seem good at times, but look at the hand that is behind those circumstances, "working" those circumstances!

We must hear the Lord speaking to our spirits, "I'm working it out. Don't judge yet. The final conclusion hasn't been revealed yet. I'm not through yet. Just keep looking at the master blueprint of My will."

That we should be to the praise of his glory, who first trusted in Christ.

EPHESIANS 1:12

As God is working all things for the highest and greatest good for all, we who have trusted in Christ should live to the praise of His glory. We are incited to continuously praise and worship and glorify Him because we are His inheritance and He has everything in our lives worked out. Now that is a truth that should cause us to start dancing! That is the master blueprint for our lives. That is the purpose of God for all who are in His Church. We are His inheritance to the praise of His glory!

UNDER CONSTRUCTION

In whom ye also trusted, after that ye heard the word of truth, the gospel of your salvation in whom also,

*after that ye believed, ye were sealed with that holy
Spirit of promise,*

*Which is the earnest of our inheritance until the
redemption of the purchased possession, unto the praise
of his glory.*

EPHESIANS 1:13-14

We can trust God. Why? Because we have heard
the word of truth, the Gospel, and believed. God's
Word is absolutely trustworthy and we can be
completely secure in Him. But this verse reveals
another more authoritative verification that our
trust in God is solid: we are sealed with the Holy
Spirit. The word seal is *sphragizo*. This word is used
in a variety of ways in Scripture. There is the seal
that is like a cap or cover, where something is
secured or fastened by a seal. An example of this
kind of seal is the stone that covered the tomb in
which Jesus was laid. A seal could also be used to keep
something secret. When God gave John a glimpse
of the future in the book of the Revelation, aspects
of what John saw were "sealed" and kept secret.

But in Ephesians 1:13, the word "seal" has a glorious
meaning. This seal is a *mark of identification*. This mark
denotes ownership and therefore protection. Even
when standing in a crowd of people, the believer
carries God the Father's mark of holy distinction.

Nevertheless the foundation of God standeth sure, having this seal, The Lord knoweth them that are his.

2 TIMOTHY 2:19

God knows those who are His. The seal He has placed on us attests, certifies, and acknowledges that we belong to God. Therefore, we enjoy His full protection. This protection covers the attacks the enemy launches against our minds and against our lives. But it is more than just an identification mark *on* us. It is a mark *in* us. For we are marked or sealed by the Holy Spirit, who is in us.

I recently had some legal work done and had a notary public put his seal on the legal document I was signing. That seal authenticated the document. It showed that the document was legitimate and that my identity was verified. The Holy Spirit in us is the *seal of God* on our lives. He is the sign to the devil that we belong to God and that we are authentically and indisputably God's. God's redemptive work in us is sealed, settled, complete, incontestable, and legitimate. Just as the Holy Spirit authenticated to Peter and the Jewish believers that the Gentiles in Cornelius' house were legitimately God's in Acts 10:34-35, the Holy Spirit authenticates that we are legitimately and irrevocably His to the devil, the world, and mankind.

The devil sees and recognizes the seal of the Holy Spirit on our lives. In Acts 19:11-20, there were some men imitating Paul by using the name of Jesus to try to cast out a demon, but they were not believers. They didn't have the seal of the Holy Spirit. So the demon said to them, "Jesus I know, and Paul I know; but who are you?" and literally tore the clothes off their backs and ran them out of town!

I would strongly suggest to you that if you haven't truly given your life to Jesus Christ, if you have not been sealed by the Holy Ghost, but you have been going to church and playing some religious game, stop it and get right with God right now! Don't mess around with the name of Jesus and the power of God, because even the devil recognizes what is legitimately and rightfully God's. You must have the powerful presence of the Holy Spirit in your life to be sealed and protected.

The text states that the Holy Spirit is also "the earnest of our inheritance." The word "earnest" in the Greek is *arrabon* and means "first installment; deposit; down payment; pledge that pays a part of the purchased price in advance, and so secures a legal claim to the article in question or makes a valid contract."

This seal of the Holy Spirit is God's holy and solemn pledge that He will redeem us completely from everything that torments us and causes us concern — past, present, and future. The Holy Spirit is God's legal claim and His valid contract signifying that He is the author and finisher of our faith and will bring us into glory with Him. The Holy Spirit is God's investment in our future. He is our empowering, our energizer and encourager who assures us we are going to make it. If the Holy Spirit, as good as He is, is just a down payment, what will the full payment be like?!!!

The down payment God gives to us must not be confused with the kind of down payment people place on houses or other property. It would be a perfect analogy if we never violated the spirit of that down payment. The concept is that our down payment should assure the seller that we fully intend to purchase the property in question. However, people routinely forfeit their down payment when they no longer have an interest in the property, or they write so many conditions into the contract that they nullify the power of their earnest money.

But it is not so with God! His down payment is a sure guarantee of more to come. Paul states that the earnest of the Holy Spirit is given to us until "the redemption of the purchased possession," or until our redemption is fully manifested. Our full redemption was purchased with the precious blood of Jesus Christ at Calvary, but the entire manifestation of that transaction will not be seen until we are in our resurrection bodies, all evil has been put away forever, and we are abiding in the new heaven and earth. John wrote in 1 John 3:2 that we are now the sons of God, "and it doth not yet *appear* what we shall be." In the meantime, we are sealed, we have the earnest, and we are under construction.

Have you ever been on a construction site? There is a point in the construction of any building when the entire project looks like a mess. There's steel and block everywhere, dirt and sand in piles, everybody is wearing hard hats and safety glasses, and the site looks like anything but a building. However, it doesn't matter how things look at that stage. The architect is there with his blueprint. He has a vision for what the place is going to look like when it's finished. And so, over time and bit by bit, under the supervision of the architect, the blocks, steel beams, wood, and piles of sand and dirt begin to be moved here and there. The building is being put together with much forethought and care. It's coming together. Although it may be days, months, or even years before there is even a hint of a structure, the building is being built.

And so it is with us. We may think we are a mess right now, and we may be a mess! If the Church is doing its work correctly, there should be lots of messy people in its midst — people who have been pulled from the messiest situations of sin imaginable and who are still in the process of being cleaned up. No baby comes out of the womb of its mother all cleaned up, and spiritual rebirthing is just as messy! But the good news is that we are spiritually reborn. We are under construction! There's a purpose and plan behind all that is going on in our lives. Things are coming together. We are a magnificent temple of the Holy Spirit under construction!

The Holy Spirit is a sign to us that we have been sealed into eternal life and God's family, that we belong to God. This should give us tremendous security! God does not just redeem us out of the marketplace to let us go free and mess up our lives according to our own wills. No! He redeems us out of the marketplace and then says, "You are free in Christ Jesus, and I am going to bring about in you the fulfillment of your life and the purpose of your life. In the process, I am going to give you the greatest joy and satisfaction and meaning you could ever know. The devil no longer has any right to wrap you in bondage, oppress you, or manipulate you. You are free in Christ Jesus and I am not going to abandon you. I am going to build you up, make you, fashion you, and mold you to be a person of high esteem, high value, and high purpose both now and in all eternity."

Let me tell you — you ought to *flaunt* the Holy Spirit in your life! Not that you have the Holy Spirit and others don't, but simply that you *have* the Holy Spirit! We are to manifest the Holy Spirit within us, stand on the fact that the Holy Spirit is working in us and through us, and allow the Holy Spirit to show the love and power of God through us to others.

Any time the devil comes against us, we should be quick to say, "Oh no, devil, I know I'm accepted in the Beloved. Oh no, devil, I know I've been redeemed by the blood. Oh no, devil, I know I've been forgiven. Oh no, devil, I know to whom I belong and why. I'm under contract and I'm under construction. I have the seal of the Holy Spirit on my life and my life is hid in Christ with God. I live by the faith of the Son of God who loved me and gave Himself a ransom for me. It is in Him that I live and move and have my being."

Any time the devil comes at me, I slap his face with about twenty-five good, hot scriptures and then I start praising God for the Holy Spirit in my life. The Holy Spirit is my seal of authentic ownership by God, and in the presence of that seal, the devil can't touch me. It doesn't really matter what I'm going through. My body might be sick, but my spirit has been sealed. My finances might be lacking, but my spirit has been sealed. And the good news is that I'm going through. I'm going THROUGH. I'm going to emerge on the other side better than ever!

The blocks and steel and dirt are being moved around so that God's highest and best purposes for my construction will be fulfilled. I'm not only going through troubles, but I'm on the way to receiving all spiritual and natural blessings in Christ Jesus — "unto the praise of his glory." Everything I am and will become, everything I have and will have, and the glorious redemption in which I am sealed by the Holy Spirit are all for one purpose: to praise Him and glorify Him. Hallelujah!

8

HOPE

Wherefore I also, after I heard of your faith in the Lord Jesus, and love unto all the saints,

Cease not to give thanks for you, making mention of you in my prayers.

EPHESIANS 1:15-16

The first chapter of Ephesians makes a turn in verse 15 when Paul begins a very lengthy, fervent, and specific prayer for the Ephesian congregation. Writing from his prison cell in Rome, he says that from the moment he heard of their conversion, he unceasingly offered thanksgiving to God for them and began praying for them. The Ephesians are standing strong! They are growing in Christ Jesus. They are manifesting faith in Jesus Christ and loving one another. And this prayer speaks again of His special, intimate, and loving relationship with them. Then, in verse 17, he begins to tell them exactly what he is praying for them and the Church at large to receive.

THE KNOWLEDGE OF HIM

That the God of our Lord Jesus Christ, the Father of glory, may give unto you the spirit of wisdom and revelation in the knowledge of him.

EPHESIANS 1:17

After introducing our masterful God, Paul makes the request to the Father of glory to give His children "the spirit of wisdom and revelation." Literally, Paul wants us to comprehend and know our magnificent God in all His wisdom, which is accomplished "in the knowledge of him." When we *know* the God of all wisdom, His wisdom becomes ours.

Many believers are quick to seek and desire more of God's power or God's love. But too few believers are quick to seek diligently for more of God's wisdom, discernment, and understanding. The wisdom and revelation of God contain all the wealth of the believer, because wisdom and revelation will reveal both God's will and His heart in any situation. Therefore, if we know God, we will know His will and His heart. In most cases, obtaining wisdom and revelation is just a matter of spending time with Him and asking Him.

*If any of you lack wisdom, let him ask of God,
who giveth to all men liberally, and upbraideth not;
and it will be given to him.*

JAMES 1:5

Liberally, abundantly, and without any reproach
or recrimination — that is the way God desires to
impart wisdom to us.

Liberally is freely and generously.

Abundantly is sufficiently and excessively.

Without reproach or recrimination is willingly
and eagerly.

The Bible tells us plainly and repeatedly how
valuable wisdom is to the believer.

*Wisdom is better than rubies; and all the things that
may be desired are not to be compared to it.*

By [wisdom] *kings reign, and princes decree justice.*

Riches and honor are with [wisdom]; *yea, durable
riches and righteousness.*

[The fruit of wisdom] *is better than gold, yea,
than fine gold; and* [the] *revenue* [of wisdom] *than
choice silver.*

Blessed are they that keep [the ways of wisdom].

For whoso findeth [wisdom] *findeth life, and
shall obtain favor of the Lord.*

PROVERBS 8:11,15,18-19,32,35

God wants us to know Him because He knows
that wisdom and revelation come in the knowledge
of Him. And believers cannot fulfill their call and

possess the joy of their salvation without wisdom and revelation. But the key to all wisdom and revelation, again, is knowing God.

Nothing is more wonderful than knowing God! Note that I did not say, knowing *about* God. Many people, even those who don't believe in Jesus Christ, know about God. *Knowing* God is something entirely different! Knowing God is having an intimate, daily, walking-and-talking relationship with Him. Knowing God is experiencing His presence in us and moving through us at all times.

At one point in his life, Paul knew about God. He knew about Jesus of Nazareth, but he didn't believe in Jesus. He held the coats of those who stoned Stephen, one of the first deacons of the church. He zealously persecuted the first Christians and was openly out for their blood. But then, as he was on his way to Damascus to persecute the Christians there, he was blinded by a bright light that literally knocked him to the ground. He heard a voice saying to him, "Saul, Saul, why persecutest thou me?" And he answered, "Who art thou, Lord?" The Lord spoke back, "I am Jesus whom thou persecutest" (Acts 9:4-5). Later Paul would write:

> **Y**ea doubtless, and I count all things but loss for the excellency of the knowledge of Christ Jesus my Lord.
>
> PHILIPPIANS 3:8

Nothing mattered to Paul, nothing was of any worth or value or significance, and all things were considered a loss to Him except knowing Jesus.

Paul was not an ignorant man. He spoke several languages, was affluent, intellectual, articulate, and a profound, prolific writer. He spoke clearly and zealously about what he believed. He was a man who could bring great order and structure to ideas. Of the tribe of Benjamin, the tribe from which kings had come, he was part of the Sanhedrin, the ruling body of Judaism. He was a man to be respected, but when he *knew* Jesus, nothing else mattered.

Paul's prayer was that the Ephesians would *know* God as He really is. He knew that if they came to the knowledge of Him, nothing else would matter to them. Their love for God would multiply exceedingly and abundantly. When we love someone, we can never know them enough. We are always wanting to grow in the knowledge of them. Although we can never know God fully, it is nevertheless our lifelong pursuit to know Him fully. He always has more of His wisdom to impart, more of His presence to bestow, more of His power to grant, and more of His love to pour into our hearts.

I have met people who know Greek and Hebrew. They know church history, church protocol, everybody's doctrine, and all theology. The question is, "Do they know God?" If they know Him, all of the rest falls in line and is of less importance. Knowing God is the greatest "knowing" of all, and the good news to every Christian is that we can know Him. He desires to reveal Himself to us!

Do you *know* Jesus today?

Do you desire to know Him even more?

ENLIGHTENMENT

The eyes of your understanding being enlightened; that ye may know what is the hope of his calling, and what the riches of the glory of his inheritance in the saints.

EPHESIANS 1:18

Imagine you are in a totally dark room when someone turns on a flashlight. The picture of that flashlight dispelling the darkness by its light describes the word "enlightened." Once the flashlight is turned on, there is no more darkness. Light has come and the room is illuminated. The tense of the verb "enlightened" suggests that we have been enlightened and continue to enjoy this illumination in the present. It is a continual process of being exposed to the illumination of God's work and will. In terms of our flashlight example, the room grows brighter as we shine the light longer and investigate all the areas of the room. When the eyes of our understanding are being enlightened, it is a grand adventure of discovering truth!

In every area of darkness in our lives — it may be the darkness of memories in the past, or it may be darkness about things with which our minds continue to struggle — the Lord's light can shine and give us understanding. Paul prays that even in the darkest cellar of the souls of the Ephesians, way down there in the nooks and crevices of their minds and emotions, the light of God's truth will shine.

You see, where the truth of God's light shines, He begins to create and to manifest His power. When God's light shines, His presence is felt, His power begins to flow, and change starts to occur. So whatever our understanding may be of a situation, a relationship, or an experience — past or present — if we pray for God's truth to shine on our understanding, His truth will illuminate our minds, and we will know all we need to know.

The work of the Holy Spirit is a work of renewal in us. We have to change our old habits — physical and emotional and mental — into new habits that line up with the Word of God. This renewal process begins with God's light of truth shining on our understanding. It is a process in which we come into greater and greater revelation and knowledge about what it means to be in Christ and to have the Holy Spirit of Christ Jesus dwelling in us.

Please note that "renewing" is not the same as revising or making something better. "Renewing" is actually causing something to become new and different, with the implication of being superior to what was there before. The concept is analogous to being a new creature in Christ Jesus. Our spirit is not improved or cleaned up when we are born again. Our spirit is made completely new by the power of the Holy Spirit.

Having our minds "renewed" or made completely new by God's Word and the illumination of the Holy Spirit is extremely important to us because the transition from being in the world to being in the kingdom of God is a drastic one. The principles and procedures of the kingdom are so different than those we were accustomed to in the world. And when we have been used to doing something a certain way and are instructed to change that habit, we need assurance and direction.

We need to know that the new methods and procedures will work for us, and God gave us that assurance by displaying His great power when He saved us. If He was loving and gracious enough to save us out of Satan's grasp and the kingdom of darkness, how much more will He do for us now that we are His children? At this revelation, our eyes seek to be enlightened and we are exposed to more and more of the glorious work of Jesus Christ. Our faith is strengthened and expanded. We discover that the more we know God, the more we trust Him in situations we have not experienced before and circumstances which have intimidated us in the past. Our faith soars and our confidence in Him becomes steadfast and immovable.

Do you know your purpose in life today? Ask the Lord to enlighten your understanding.

Do you know why certain things are happening to you today? Ask the Lord to enlighten your understanding.

Do you know the source of turmoil behind certain circumstances or situations? Ask the Lord to enlighten your understanding.

Are you depressed, troubled, or worried today? Ask the Lord to enlighten your understanding.

God wants you to know Him so that you can know how to deal with any given situation in life. He has chosen to reveal to you what unbelievers cannot know and what the prophets of old were not allowed to know. (See 1 Peter 1:12.) What is even more fascinating is that the phrase "that you might know" is not meant to suggest an academic knowing or a self-help knowing. The word in the original

Greek text is not *ginosko*, "to possess information about," but it is *oida*, which means "to be intimately acquainted with, to stand in a close relation to something." God wants you to be intimately acquainted with "the hope of his calling, and what the riches of the glory of his inheritance in the saints."

LIFE WITHOUT END

To hope is to believe God has prepared a future for us. Not only have we been chosen for a purpose in the here and now, not only are we loved, redeemed, forgiven, and given access to unlimited wisdom and revelation, but we have been given the great gift of eternity! As believers in Christ Jesus, our future stretches into forever. Our life has no end.

> **F**or I know the thoughts that I think toward you, saith the Lord, thoughts of peace, and not of evil, to give you an expected end.
>
> JEREMIAH 29:11

In the *New King James Version*, this verse concludes, "to give you a future and a hope."

God's plan for us doesn't end in this lifetime.

God's purposes for us are not bound to this earth.

God has an eternal plan and purpose for our lives.

The more we see Jesus, and the more our understanding is enlightened by Jesus, the greater our hope for the future. Why? Because we realize that Jesus is in our future as much as He is in our present. The more we know Jesus, the more we are going to recognize that we cannot fail in this life, because God has destined us for eternal life with Him. We are never going to be separated from Jesus Christ. We will live with Him forever. We are joint heirs with Him. We will reign with Him.

The great comfort we receive from hope lies in the fact that we are never going to be alone or without purpose, provision, or life. We are in Christ now and forever. And once that understanding comes to us, we are going to be more and more willing to perform great exploits for the kingdom of God.

We are going to dare to be who God created us to be.

We are going to dare to speak the name of Jesus more and more, in every situation and in every circumstance of our lives.

We are going to dare to manifest the Holy Spirit to a greater and greater extent as we carry out our daily responsibilities.

The more we walk in the hope of our calling in Christ Jesus — literally the everyday consciousness of eternal life — the more we will be bold in using the power God gives to us. Hope allows us to take the risks necessary to accomplish great things, receive great blessings, and have great influence in bringing others to Jesus Christ. We have been enlightened to the hope that no matter what happens to us, we belong to God forever!

9
POWER

Wherefore I also, after I heard of your faith in the Lord Jesus, and love unto all the saints,

Cease not to give thanks for you, making mention of you in my prayers;

That the God of our Lord Jesus Christ, the Father of glory, may give unto you the spirit of wisdom and revelation in the knowledge of him:

The eyes of your understanding being enlightened; that ye may know what is the hope of his calling, and what the riches of the glory of his inheritance in the saints.

EPHESIANS 1:15-18

Paul is praying for us to receive all wisdom and revelation as we grow in the knowledge of God more and more, for the light to expand in our hearts and minds so we might grasp the reality of our hope in God's eternal plan and purpose for our lives. Then, when we think our souls will burst with the vastness of all God has provided for us, we are bombarded with power words.

FIVE WORDS TO PACK A PUNCH

> **A**nd what is the exceeding greatness of his power to usward who believe, according to the working of his mighty power.
>
> EPHESIANS 1:19

In verse 19 alone, Paul uses five different words to describe the vast power of God which is placed at our disposal as His children. The word translated "exceeding" is *huperballon,* which means "a throwing beyond," and depicts something that is far beyond our wildest expectations. What is being thrown beyond our wildest expectations? The greatness of God's power. This first "power" is the Greek word *dunamis,* which means "inherent power." Inherent means that it is in our possession but waiting for our signal to be released or activated.

Let's return to our example of the Hoover Dam, a wall of concrete which controls the flow of trillions of tons of water. When all of the outlets for water are closed, we see that the dam continues to possess the ability and has the inherent power and potential to unleash an incredibly massive and powerful body of water into the Colorado River.

Inherent power is potential, always ready for the signal to be released. And Paul says that the inherent power of God is beyond our imagining!

Immediately after Paul gives us a glimpse of the vast potential power we possess in Christ Jesus, he goes with "the working of his mighty power." In the Greek text, "working" is the word *energeia*, from which we derive the word energy. *Energeia* speaks of energy that is being expended, exercised, and put into full operation. And what, exactly, is being expended? His mighty power!

"Mighty" is *ischus* and "power" is *kratos* in the Greek. *Ischus* is raw strength and literally an endowment of physical prowess. *Kratos* is manifested strength, might, or power. Paul is giving us a multiple portion of power in this one verse of Scripture! Why do you think the Holy Spirit is leading him to do this? Because He wants us to get a revelation of the massive power available to us when we simply believe and act upon God's Word. His power is made available toward "us who believe." All of those who come through the door of faith have access to the full and exceeding greatness and limitlessness of God's power!

God has unlimited ability to get us out of trouble. He has unlimited resources for making sure that we can do all that He has called us to do. He has unlimited capacity for taking us from where we are to where He desires us to be. Furthermore, He is continually looking for opportunities to display and operate in power on our behalf.

RESURRECTION POWER

> **A**nd what is the exceeding greatness of his power to usward who believe, according to the working of his mighty power,
>
> Which he wrought in Christ, when he raised him from the dead, and set him at his own right hand in the heavenly places.
>
> EPHESIANS 1:19-20

In the Old Testament, the "exceeding greatness" of God's power was manifested when He parted the Red Sea and the Israelites were saved from the armies of Pharaoh. Even today in the Passover celebration, God reminds the Jews of His power by saying, "Am I not the God who brought you across the Red Sea?" It was in crossing the Red Sea that they were supernaturally delivered from their enemy.

For the believer, the "exceeding greatness" of God's power is displayed in the resurrection of Jesus Christ from the dead. These verses say that God "wrought" His power in Christ at the resurrection, and the word "wrought" is another power word. It means "to actively prove oneself strong." Now God did not just prove Himself strong at the resurrection of Jesus. He proved Himself stronger than any force or being in the universe! It is because of the resurrection that we are delivered from Satan, the power of death, and all evil. When Jesus rose from the dead and took the sting out of death and victory out of the grave, He proved forever that He was and is the Lord of *all* things, not just the Lord of *some* things.

As the Jews refer again and again to their deliverance from Egypt at the parting of the Red Sea, Christians must never tire of recalling the resurrection of Jesus Christ.

It is the resurrection that assures us of our salvation.

It is in the resurrection that we have our greatest hope — eternal life.

It is the resurrection that reveals the fullness of the power of God toward us.

It is in recalling the resurrection that our faith in God is made secure.

Is there any power greater than the power to restore life to something that is completely and totally dead? God alone imparts *resurrection power.*

Resurrection power causes dead things to live again.

Resurrection power causes temporal things to become eternal things.

And resurrection power is made available to us!

Let this truth about God's power sink deep into your spirit. What is it that seems dead to you today but which you know God desires to see alive and whole? Is your marriage dead? Is your professional life dead in the water? Is your credit rating dead on arrival? Is your creativity dead from too many rejections? Is your heart dead from too much heartache or sorrow? Is your witness dead from fear? Is your peace dead from turmoil and torment?

God causes dead things to live again just as surely as He caused Jesus to be resurrected from the dead. And God not only causes dead things to live, but He brings them into wholeness and endows them with eternal purpose. This is a critically important aspect of God's gift to you that you must understand. God not only gives life, but He gives *meaning* to life. God not only produces quantity of life and quality of life, but He gives *eternal purpose* to life.

Once you begin to see your marriage as something God can cause to come alive again and something which has eternal meaning and significance before God, you are going to want your marriage to be restored and to be vibrant with love.

Once you see that talent lying dormant within you as something which God wants to see come alive and you begin to see that the use of your talent has eternal purpose and importance to God, you are going to want to dust off that talent and start developing it and using it.

Once you see that God wants your paralyzed and disappointed heart to come alive and express love to people so they can be saved and healed and live forever in heaven, you are going to want to start loving again, even if it means being vulnerable and taking a risk.

God is the victor over death and the grave because He has unlimited power to resurrect and He gives eternal meaning to all aspects of our lives. His power cannot be quenched. He is omnipotent and all powerful. There is nothing so dead or so insignificant that He cannot bring it to life and give it eternal purpose.

ULTIMATE AUTHORITY

Which he wrought in Christ, when he raised him from the dead, and set him at his own right hand in the heavenly places,

Far above all principality, and power, and might, and dominion, and every name that is named, not only in this world, but also in that which is to come:

And hath put all things under his feet, and gave him to be the head over all things to the church,

Which is his body, the fulness of him that filleth all in all.

EPHESIANS 1:20-23

When God resurrected Jesus from the dead, He didn't stop there. He sat Jesus at His right hand, and to be seated at the right hand of the Creator of the Universe is to be seated in the place of all authority. It is one thing to understand and know about the power of God, but it is quite another to have the *authority* to use and operate in His power. God didn't just display all His power when He raised Jesus from the dead, but He also seated Jesus at His right hand to symbolize that all of His power was now subject to the authority of Jesus, His Son.

Obviously, God's throne is in heaven, and this passage of Scripture makes it clear that the throne of God is far above any other authority or power in existence. Paul lists the specific powers and authorities over which Jesus has rule:

Principality — *arche*, which means "a first one, a leader." This word generally refers to spirit beings, either angelic or demonic, who have rulership.

Power — *exousia*, which means "delegated authority." *Exousia* is the power that principalities or spiritual leaders wield.

Might — *dunamis*, which means "inherent power." As discussed before, *dunamis* is potential power.

Dominion — *kuriotes*, which means "lordship." *Kuriotes* speaks of a being who has rule over a territory.

Every name — Paul uses the all-inclusive "every name that is named, not only in this world, but also in that which is to come." The Greek word translated "name" is a very interesting one. It is *onoma*, and it implies that this is a name which has authority or fame.

The bully down the street may have a reputation for being tough in your neighborhood, but he is still subject to the name of Jesus!

The celebrities of this world may think they have it all under their control, but they are still subject to the authority of Jesus!

The angelic host of heaven — and one angel alone slew the entire army of Sennacherib, the enemy of Israel, in one night (see 2 Kings 19:35) — are still subject to the authority of Jesus!

Even the named angels in the Bible, Gabriel and Michael, are subject to the name of Jesus!

No matter how famous or infamous you are, you are still subject to the authority and power of Jesus Christ. Name any form of power or might in the natural realm or in the spirit realm — satanic forces, angelic beings, military might, terrorists, assassins, diseases, plagues, explosive devices, weather patterns, geological formations — and God's power is greater. Not only every form of influence, power, or authority; but every human being and every material object in creation is subject to God's resurrection power.

> **A**nd hath put all things under his feet, and gave him to be the head over all things to the church,
> Which is his body, the fulness of him that filleth all in all.

EPHESIANS 1:22-23

Paul uses a very forceful word for "hath put," *hupotasso*, which literally means "to set things in order under someone." God has not just made every person and every thing subject to the authority of Jesus Christ. He has set us in order by the authority of Jesus Christ. Everyone and everything in the created world is under the feet of, the authority of, and set in order by Jesus Christ.

The problems you are having with your family are under His feet. Jesus has order for your home.

The problems in your career are under His feet. Jesus has order for your talents, abilities, and dreams.

The corruption all around you is under His feet. Jesus has order for the world around you.

Paul also reminded the Ephesians that God "gave him to be the head over all things to the church." I discovered recently that when numbers are added in the Greek mathematical system, the sum is put at the top instead of the bottom. While we might say that Jesus is the "bottom line," the Greek system says, Jesus is the "top line." He is the sum total of the whole equation of life and all things related to the Church. When everything is added up, the answer is "Jesus." God has given Jesus as a gift to the Church. We are the most privileged class of people ever assembled in the history of mankind because we have as our leader and head the Lord Jesus Christ.

In Jesus Christ, no weapon formed against us shall prosper!

In Jesus Christ, we have authority over all the power of the enemy!

In Jesus Christ, we are locked into the limitless, universe-shaking power of God!

10

CONCLUSION:
ALL IN ALL

*And hath put all things under his feet, and gave
him to be the head over all things to the church,*
*Which is his body, the fulness of him that filleth all in
all.*

EPHESIANS 1:22-23

Verse 23 ends the first chapter of Ephesians with
a revelation of the relationship between Jesus as the
Head of the Church and the Church as His body.
This scripture sums up all the wealth we have
discovered in Christ Jesus. In the natural human
being, the head always commands the body, but in
the spiritual reality of the body of Christ, Jesus is
much more than our commander. He is our life! His
life and essence literally flow through us as He
guides and directs us and we submit to His will. In
every sense, we are one.

Literally, "the fulness of him that filleth all in all"
means that the fullness of Jesus fills the Church.
We are filled by Him. He is continually being to us

all that we need, hope, or dream. We have everything and can become all that Jesus is. He completes us with His love, moves us by His compassion, directs us with His wisdom, and empowers us with His resurrection power and authority.

As I said in the introduction to this book, Jesus is everything a human being could ever dream of, hope for, or desire — and more.

He is God's grace and glory expressed toward us and through us.

Through Him all spiritual blessings pour into our lives.

In Him we are chosen and predestined, made holy, without blame, adopted as His children, accepted in the Beloved, redeemed, and forgiven.

In Him the mystery of God's eternal will and purpose is made known to us — the reconciliation of all things in Christ Jesus.

In Him we are God's personal treasure and inheritance, sealed by the Holy Spirit and belonging solely to Him.

In Him we grow in the knowledge of God to possess His wisdom and revelation.

In Him the eyes of our understanding are enlightened and our eternal hope and calling are made sure.

In Him we have authority over every evil force opposing God and His children.

And finally, Jesus is the one who "filleth all in all." This literally means that Jesus uses all the resources of heaven and earth to fill us up to overflowing spiritually, mentally, emotionally, socially, and physically. There is nothing He cannot and will not do to see His body succeed in storming the gates of hell and possessing the land for God.

After studying Ephesians, chapter 1, there can be no doubt in our hearts and minds that we are wealthy beyond all earthly concept of wealth. There is no amount of money equal to redemption, eternal life, and all spiritual blessings — but there was a value placed upon all of this wealth by God. He deemed our wealth to be worthy of the blood of Jesus. And so the Lamb was slain from before the foundation of the world for us, not because of us. He was given because, for some incredibly awesome and unfathomable reason, God wanted you and me.

REFERENCES

Adam Clarke Commentary. 6 vols. Adam Clarke. *PC Study Bible.* Version 2.1J. CD-ROM. Seattle: Biblesoft, 1993-1998.

Barnes' Notes on the OT & NT. 14 vols. Albert Barnes. *PC Study Bible.* Version 2.1J. CD-ROM. Seattle: Biblesoft, 1993-1998.

The Bible Knowledge Commentary: An Exposition of the Scriptures. Dallas Seminary faculty. Editors, John F. Walvoord, Roy B. Zuck. Wheaton, IL: Victor Books. 1983-1985. Published in electronic form by Logos Research Systems Inc., 1996.

Brown, Driver, & Briggs' Definitions. Francis Brown, D.D., D. Litt., S. R. Driver, D.D., D. Litt., and Charles A. Briggs, D.D., D. Litt. *PC Study Bible.* Version 2.1J. CD-ROM. Seattle: Biblesoft, 1993-1998.

Expositor's Bible Commentary, New Testament. Frank E. Gaebelein, General Editor. J. D. Douglas, Associate Editor. Grand Rapids, MI: Zondervan Publishing House, 1976-1992.

A Greek-English Lexicon of the New Testament and Other Early Christian Literature. Walter Bauer. Second edition, revised and augmented by F. W. Gingrich, Fredrick Danker from Walter Bauer's fifth edition. Chicago and London: The University of Chicago Press, 1958.

The Greek New Testament. Editor Kurt Aland, et al. CD-ROM of the 3rd edition, corrected. Federal Republic of Germany: United Bible Societies, 1983. Published in electronic form by Logos Research Systems, Inc. 1996.

Greek (UBS) text and Hebrew (BHS) text. PC Study Bible. Version 2.1J. CD-ROM. Seattle: Biblesoft, 1993-1998.

The Hebrew-Greek Key Study Bible. Compiled and edited by Spiros Zodhiates, Th.D. World Bible Publishers, Inc., 1984, 1991.

Interlinear Bible. PC Study Bible. Version 2.1J. CD-ROM Seattle: Biblesoft, 1993-1998.

Jamieson, Fausset & Brown Commentary. 6 vols. Robert Jamieson, A. R. Fausset, and David Brown. *PC Study Bible.* Version 2.1J. CD-ROM. Seattle: Biblesoft, 1993-1998.

A Manual Grammar of the Greek New Testament. H. E. Dana, Th.D. and Julius R. Mantey. Toronto, Canada: MacMillan Publishing Company, 1927.

Matthew Henry's Commentary. 6 vols. Matthew Henry. *PC Study Bible.* Version 2.1J. CD-ROM. Seattle: Biblesoft, 1993-1998.

The New Linguistic and Exegetical Key to the Greek New Testament. Fritz Reineker, Revised version by Cleon Rogers and Cleon Rogers III. Grand Rapids, MI: Zondervan Publishing Company, 1998.

Strong's Exhaustive Concordance of the Bible. J. B. Strong. *PC Study Bible.* Version 2.1J. CD-ROM. Seattle: Biblesoft, 1993-1998.

Vincent's Word Studies in the NT. 4 vols. Marvin R. Vincent, D.D. *PC Study Bible.* Version 2.1J. CD-ROM. Seattle: Biblesoft, 1993-1998.

Wuest's Word Studies from the Greek New Testament for the English Reader. Volume One, Ephesians. Kenneth S. Wuest. Grand Rapids, MI: Wm. B. Eerdmans Publishing Company, 1953.

T. D. Jakes is the founder and senior pastor of The Potter's House church in Dallas, Texas. A highly celebrated author with several best-selling books to his credit, he frequently ministers in massive crusades and conferences across the nation. His weekly television broadcast is viewed nationally in millions of homes. Bishop Jakes lives in Dallas with his wife, Serita, and their five children.

To contact T. D. Jakes, write:
T. D. Jakes Ministries
International Communications Center
P. O. Box 210887
Dallas, Texas 75211

or visit his website at:
www.tdjakes.org

Loose That Man and Let Him Go!

(special gift edition)

Just for Men!

Includes 64 inspiring and motivational devotions written specifically for men. The perfect gift for any man—any time of the year.

AP-086
$16.99

Woman Thou Art Loosed

(special gift edition)

Great "anytime" gift for any woman!

The bestselling devotional, now in an exquisite cloth-bound gift edition! Daily devotions developed from the bestselling book by T. D. Jakes. The perfect gift for every woman, this cherished volume of hope and expectancy will be treasured and lovingly passed on for generations to come.

AP-085
$16.99

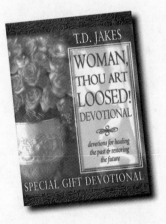

Six Pillars for the Believer *(video 1)*

First in the Series

In chapter one of Ephesians, The Apostle Paul helps us discover who we are, whose we are, what we have, and how to receive all the spiritual blessings that God has prepared for us as His children.
AP-146
$19.99

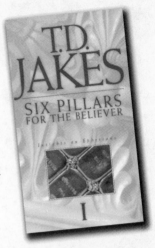

Six Pillars for the Believer *(video 2)*

Second in the Series

In chapter two of Ephesians, The Apostle Paul teaches us about our resurrection out of sin and death and how we can learn to walk with Christ in fullness of joy. Bishop Jakes encourages us to help others receive the wealth and blessing of God.
AP-147
$19.99

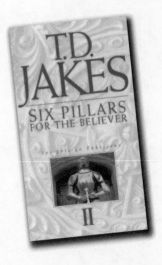

Six Pillars for the Believer *(video 3)*

Third in the Series

In chapter three of Ephesians, Paul gives us a brief autobiography. We learn in this chapter that Paul considers himself a slave for Christ. Bishop Jakes gives tremendous insight into Paul's background and holds him up as an example of forsaking self and focusing on Christ.

AP-148
$19.99

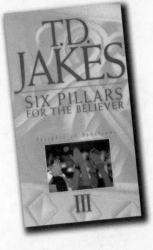

Six Pillars for the Believer *(video 4)*

Fourth in the Series

In chapter four of Ephesians, Paul shows us how to pursue the calling that God has for each of us, and he motivates us to move on to the next level. Bishop Jakes exhorts us, saying our walk as believers should be a divine reflection of our unique calling.

AP-149
$19.99

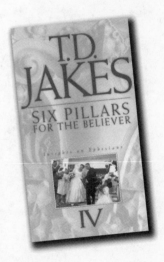

Six Pillars for the Believer *(video 5)*

Fifth in the Series

In chapter five of Ephesians, Paul challenges us to not just walk in love, but to follow Christ's example and love others just as He loved us. Bishop Jakes points out that Paul's desire was for Christians to demonstrate outwardly what God had done inwardly.
AP-150
$19.99

Six Pillars for the Believer *(video 6)*

Sixth in the Series

In chapter six of Ephesians, Paul deals with our relationships with others and how we are to submit ourselves to God and to others. Bishop Jakes speaks in depth on God's desire concerning how we manage our own house and gives several powerful principles for parents.
AP-151
$19.99

T.D. Jakes Speaks to Men

Power-Packed Quotes for Men

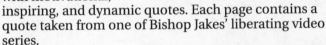

T.D. Jakes' portable for men is packed with motivational, inspiring, and dynamic quotes. Each page contains a quote taken from one of Bishop Jakes' liberating video series.
AP-986
$6.99

T.D. Jakes Speaks to Women

Life-Changing Quotes for Women

As you read each quote in this inspirational portable, you will be challenged, comforted, healed, and set free! Bishop Jakes' message is clear—that no matter where you have been or what you have done, God has forgiven you and wants to heal your past so you can change your future.
AP-987
$6.99

Lay Aside the Weight

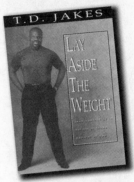

T.D. Jakes shares the way to a new you!

Discover the same nutritional, weight-loss secrets and discipline techniques that Bishop Jakes incorporated into his life. Take control! Using the five steps outlined in this dynamic book, you will learn how to shed unwanted weight in every area of your life. Includes a complete section of weight-fighting recipes!
AP-035
$19.99

Lay Aside the Weight
(workbook & journal)

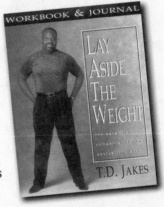

Step by Step!

The best way to get the most out of T.D. Jakes' bestselling book, *Lay Aside the Weight,* is to make it applicable to your own life. Now it's even easier to do just that! This extensive workbook and journal enables you to focus on the specific health information you need to be completely successful in your health and weight-loss plan.
AP-083
$11.99

Woman Thou Art Loosed

*The One
That Started it All!*

This book has changed hundreds of thousands of women and continues to grow in popularity. This beautiful hardcover edition makes a great gift for a loved one, friend, or even you!
AP-985
$19.99

Woman, Thou Art Loosed! *(devotional)*

*Bestseller now a
Devotional*

This insightful devotional was created for the thousands of women from around the world that have received healing and restoration through the *Woman, Thou Art Loosed!* message. Each liberating chapter is designed to assist you in keeping the binding chains of the past from refastening themselves in your life.
AP-020
$13.99

So You Call Yourself a Man?

*Bestselling
Devotional for Men*

Written in the charismatic
style that T.D. Jakes is know
for, this devotional for men
continues to be a bestseller
year after year. Be
challenged through the lives
of ordinary men in the Bible
who became extraordinary, and let
God use your life to accomplish
extraordinary things.
AP-026
$12.99

Loose that Man & Let Him Go! *(paperback)*

Over 250,000 sold!

Within the pages of this book
begins the healing of fathers
and sons. God's Word will
release the empty, nagging
ache of unresolved conflicts,
and men will learn how to
turn their pressures into
power as they bask in the
revelation light of God's plan.
AP-915
$13.99

ANCHOR PUBLISHING
P.O. Box 94002
Oklahoma 231-28 Pages

For example, if a protoflies
and is now available
www.publishing.livings.com

For international and institutional orders
please contact

Anchor Sales International
9930 East 31st Street
Suite 100
Tulsa, Oklahoma 74146
Toll Free 1-888-254-5411